This Book Belongs To

Name : _____

Phone : _____

Address : _____

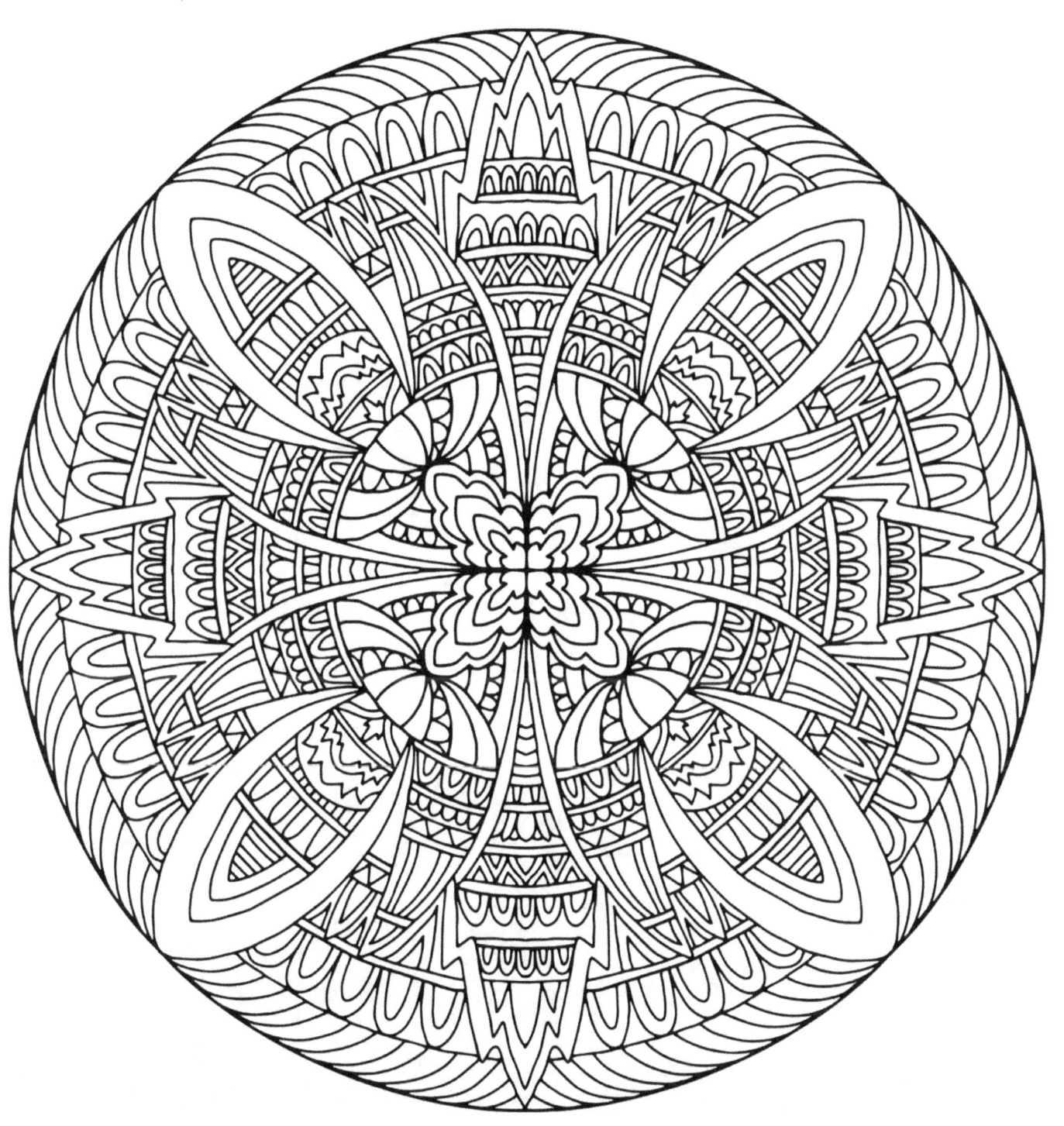

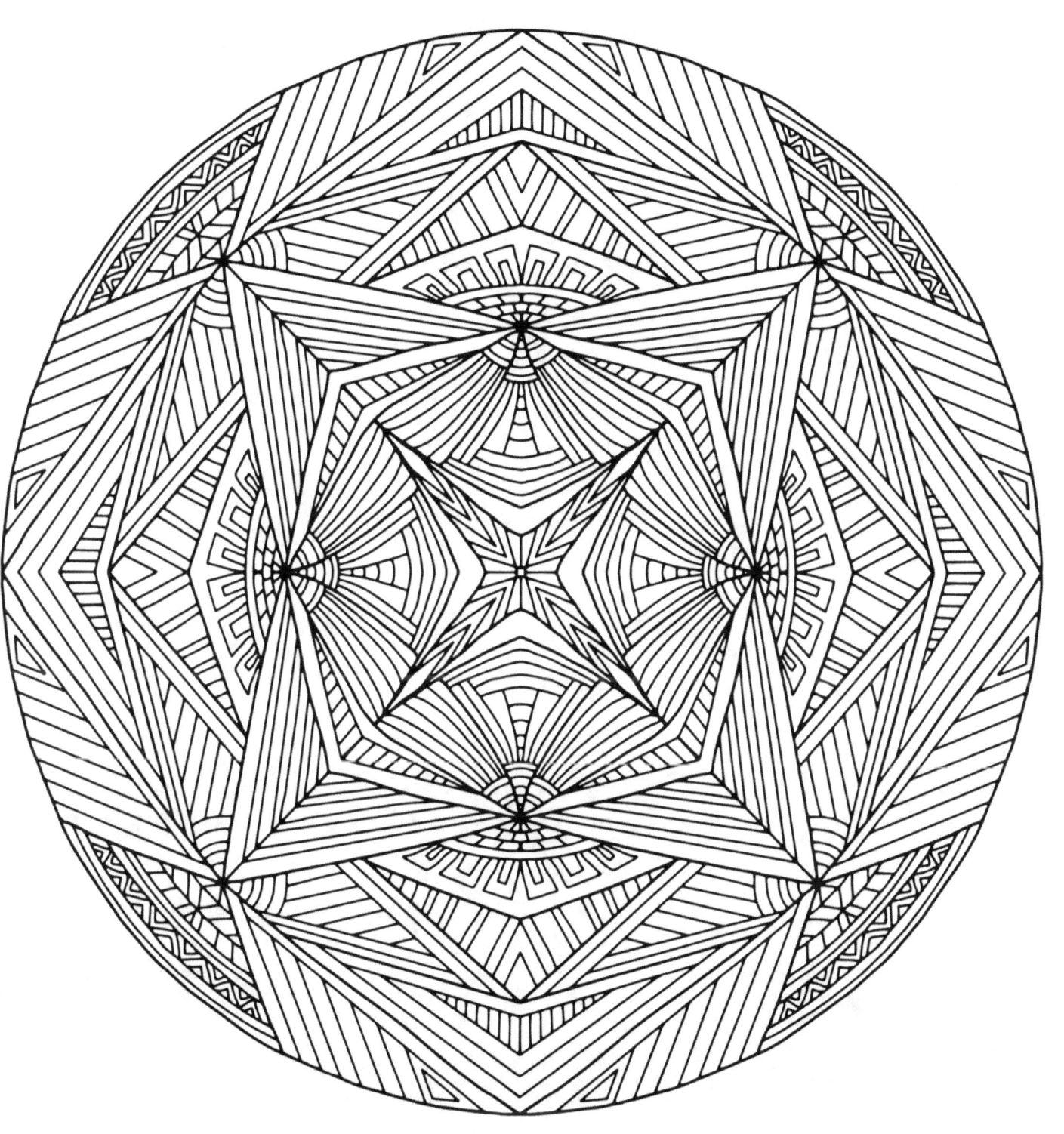

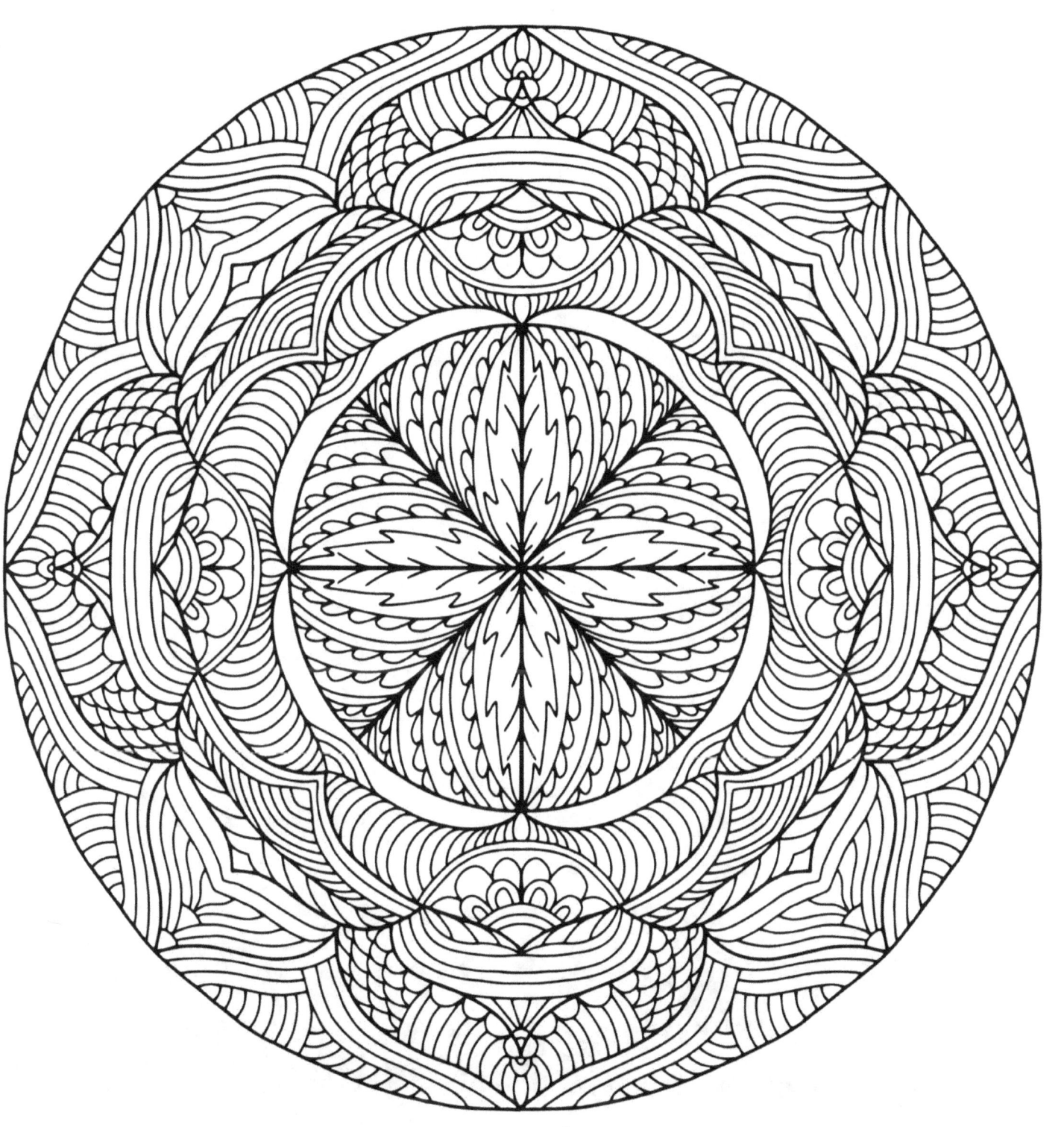

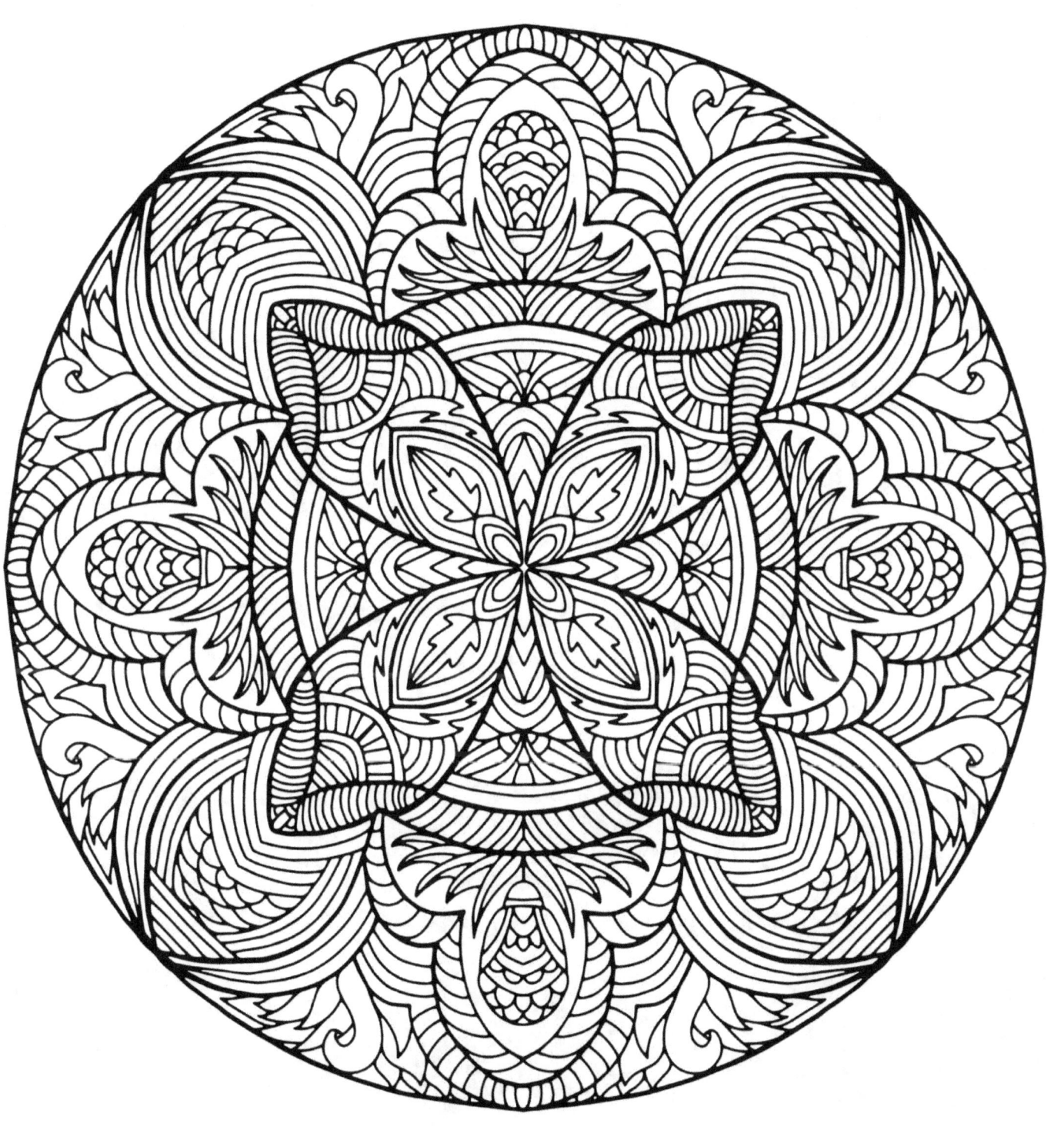

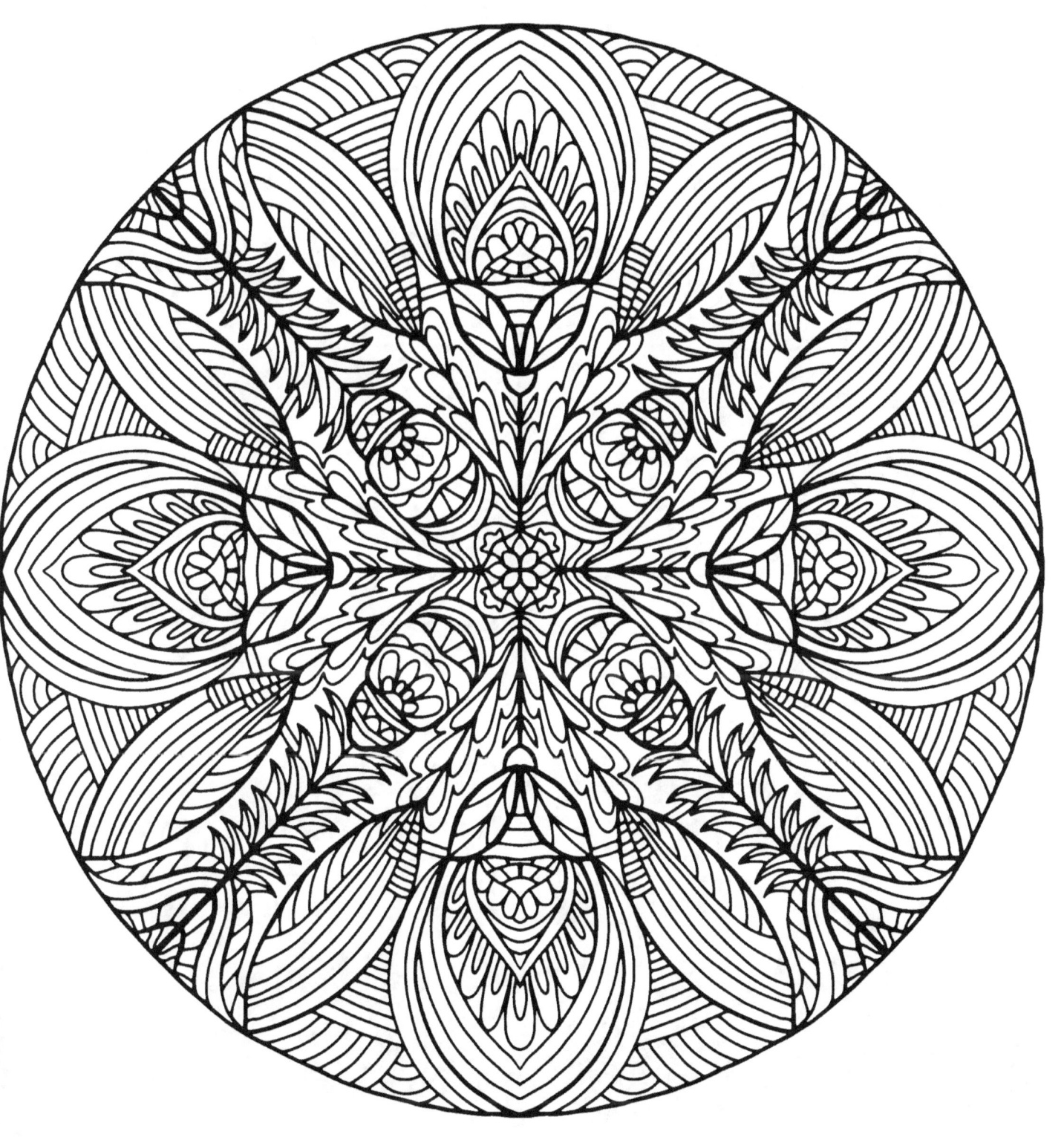

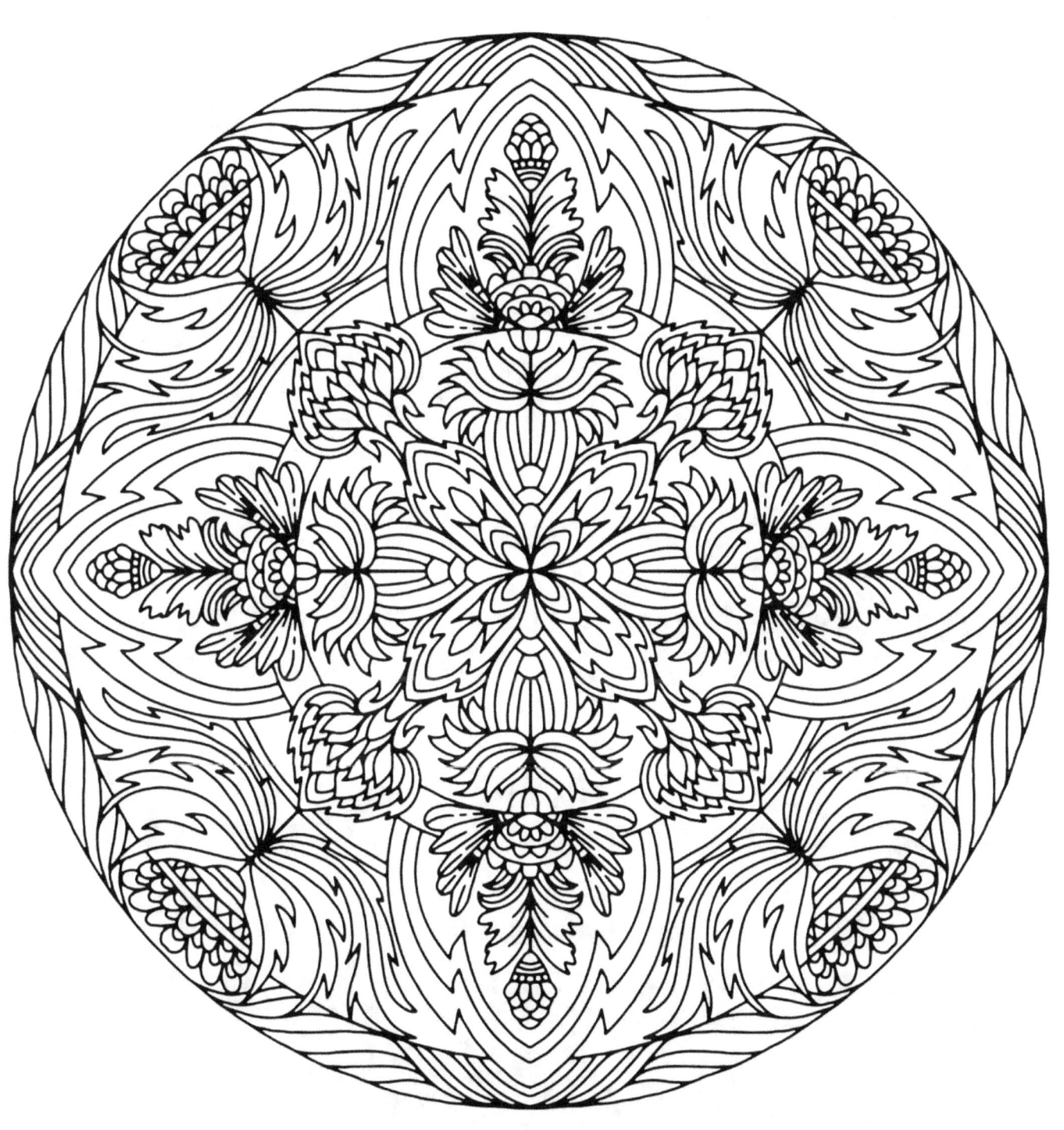

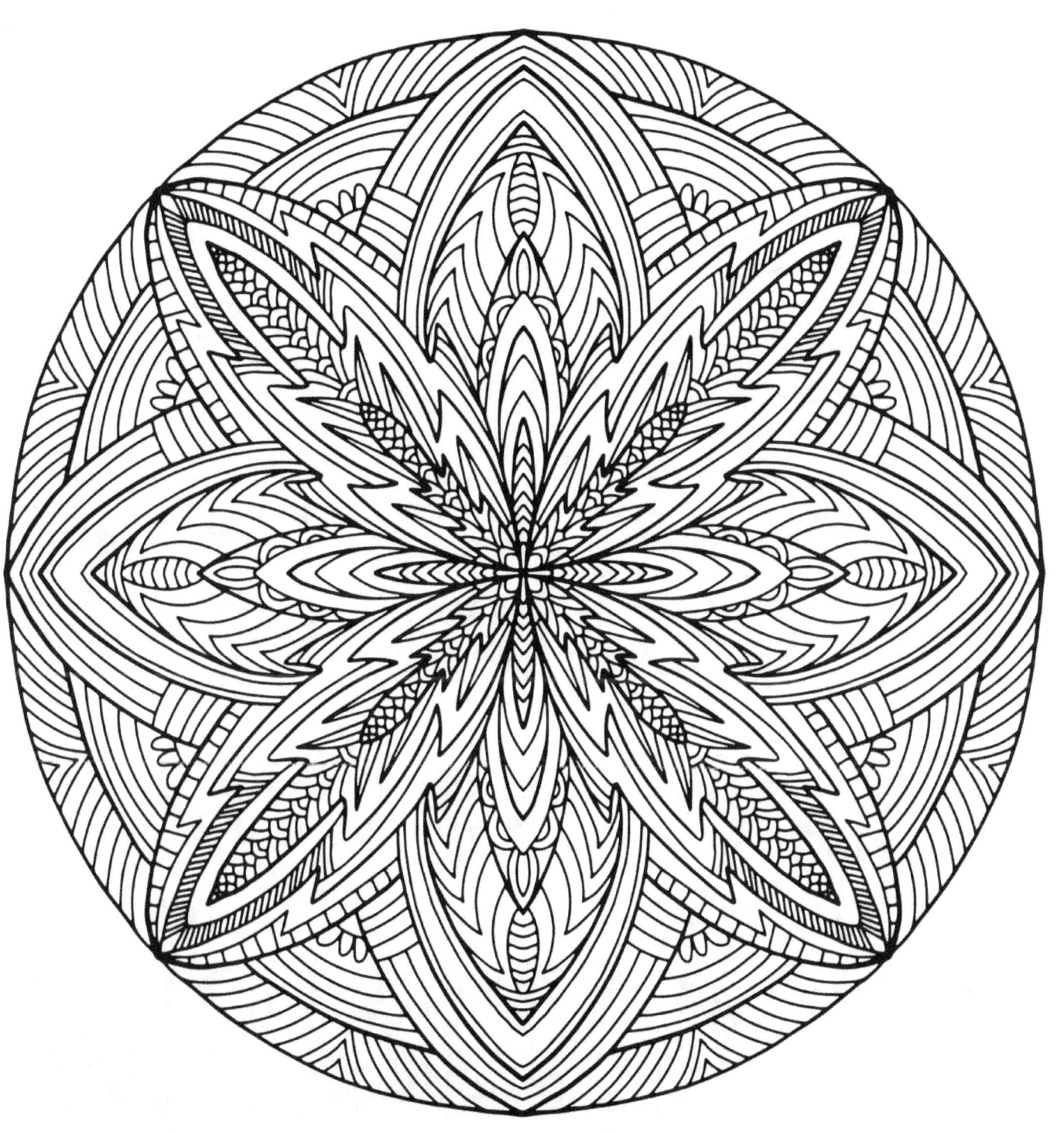

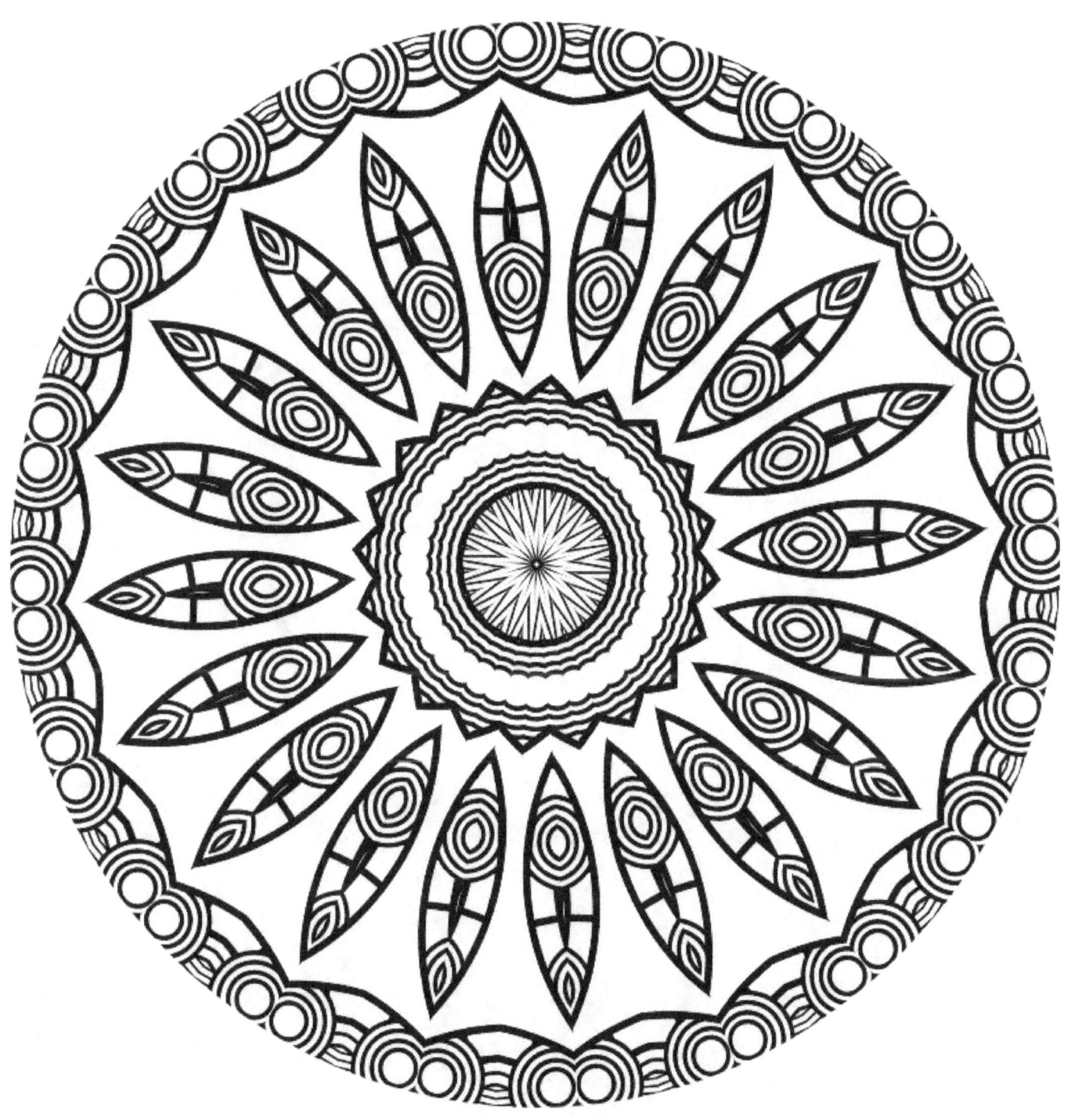

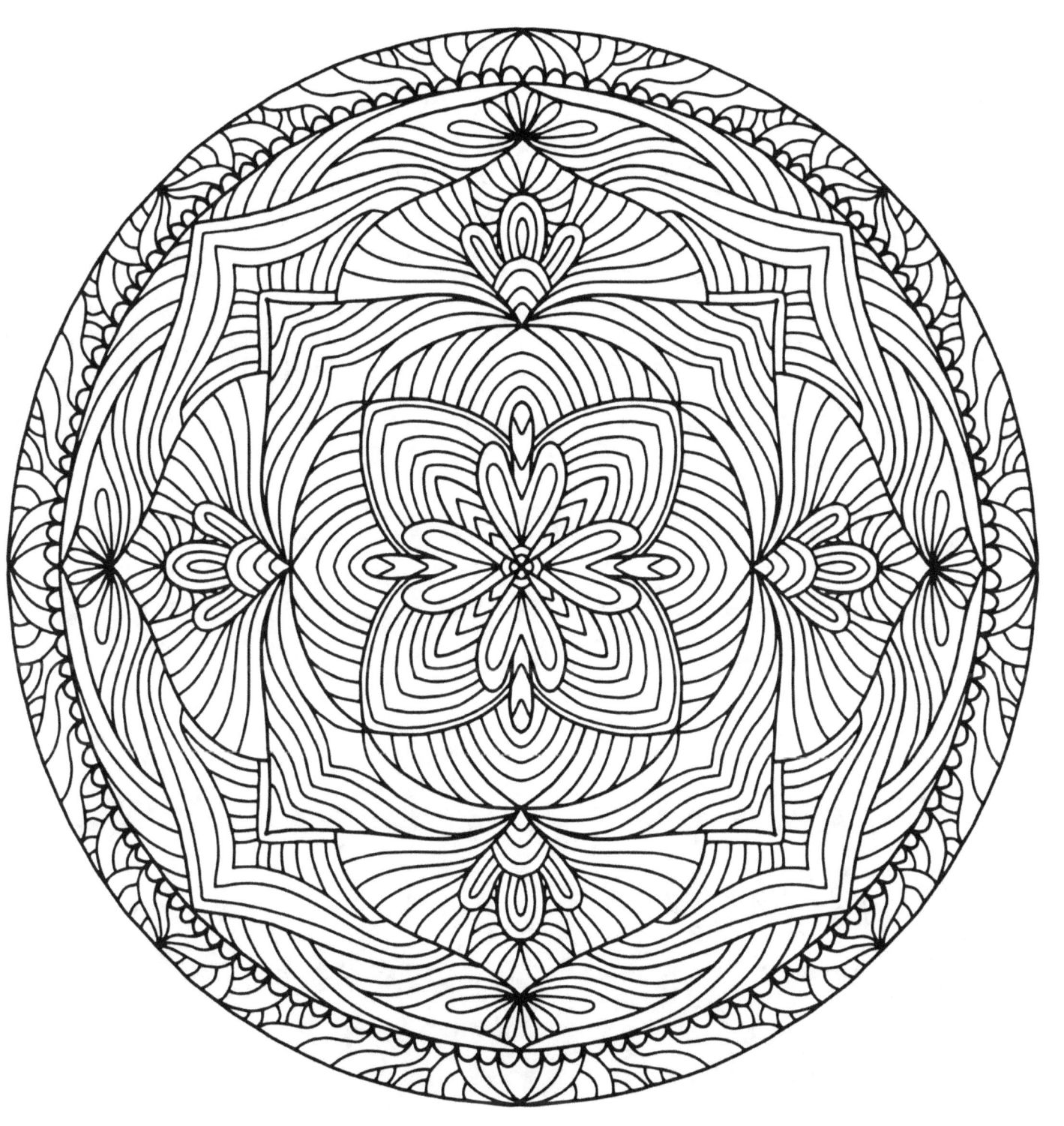

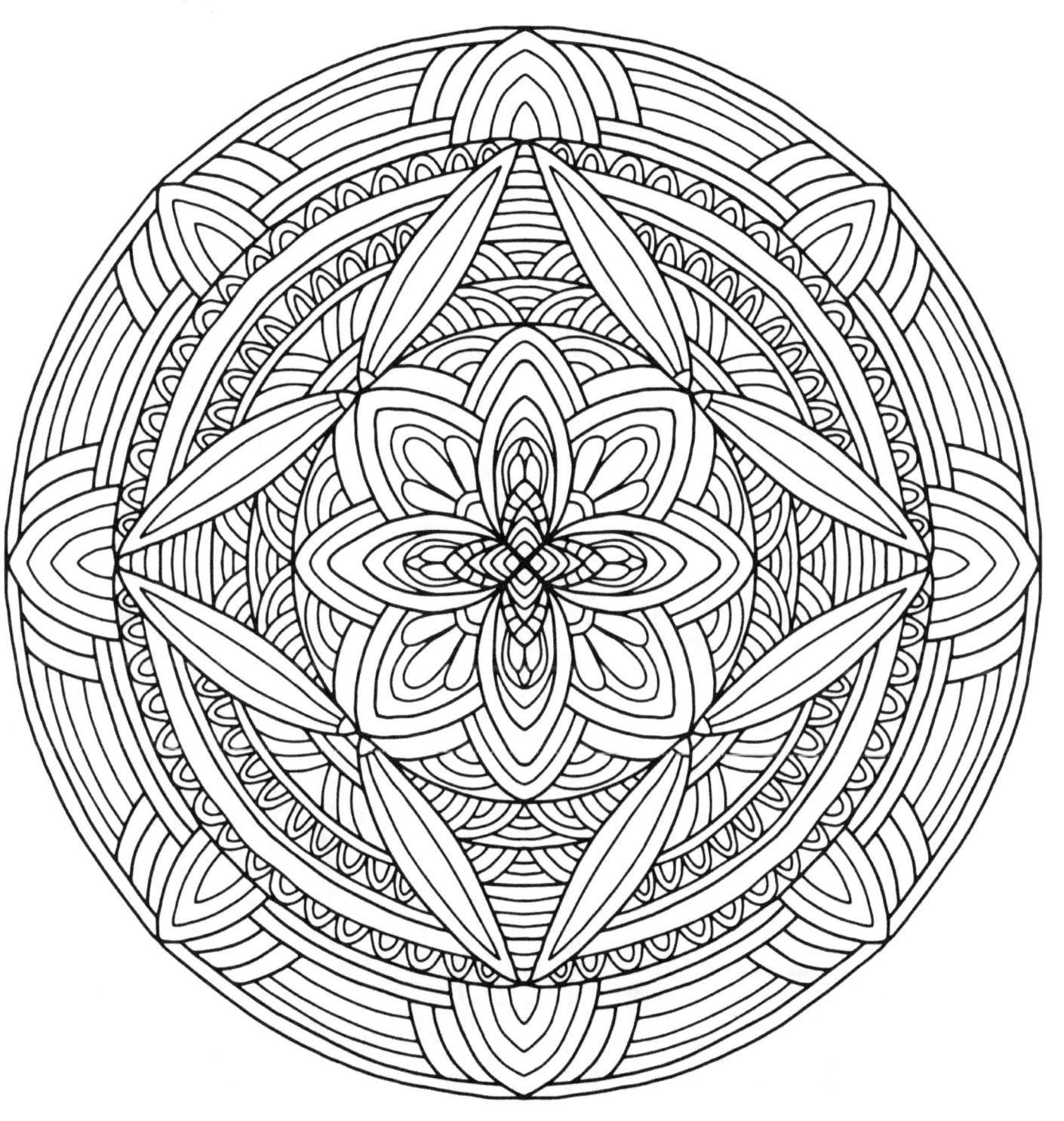

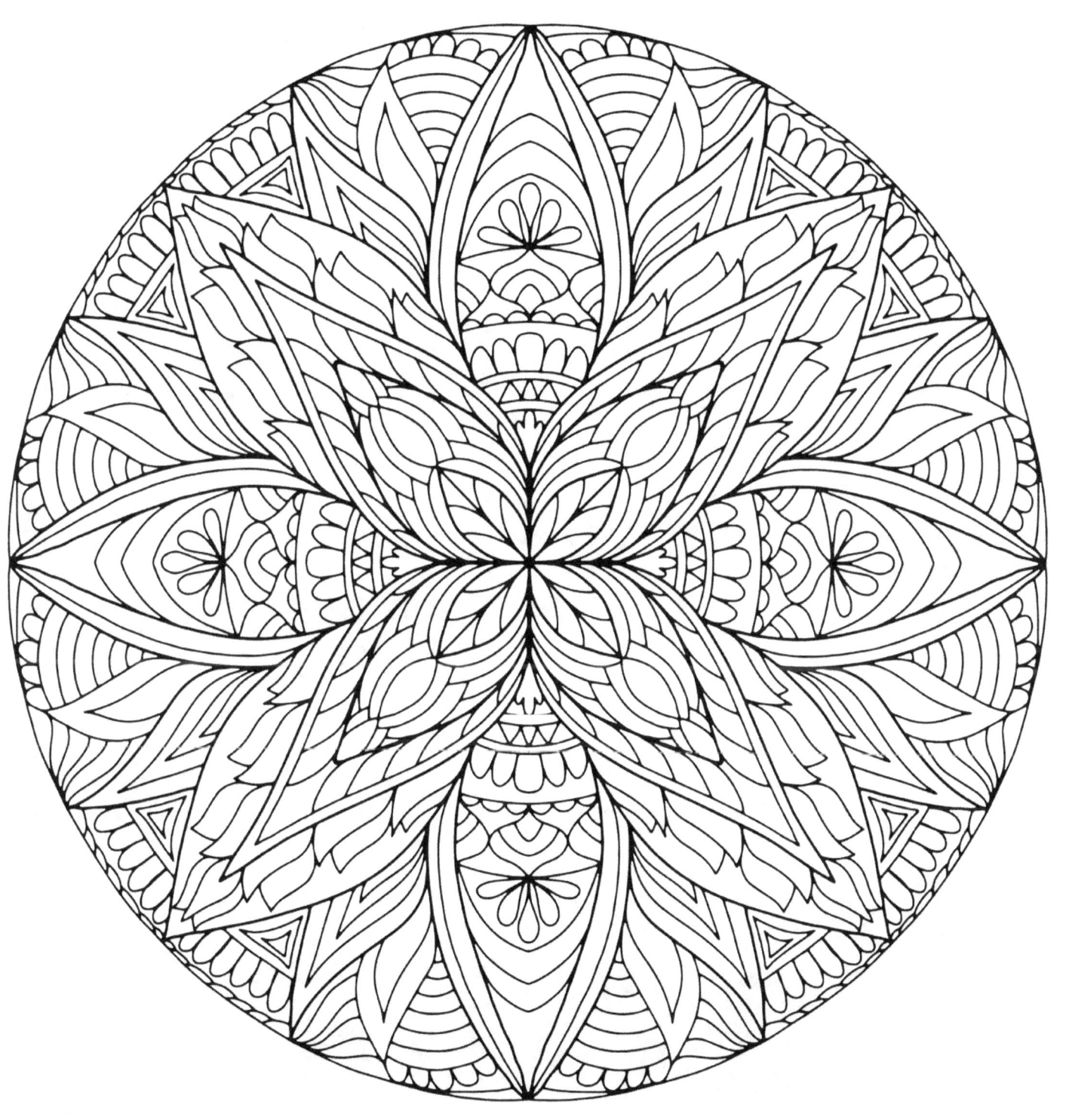

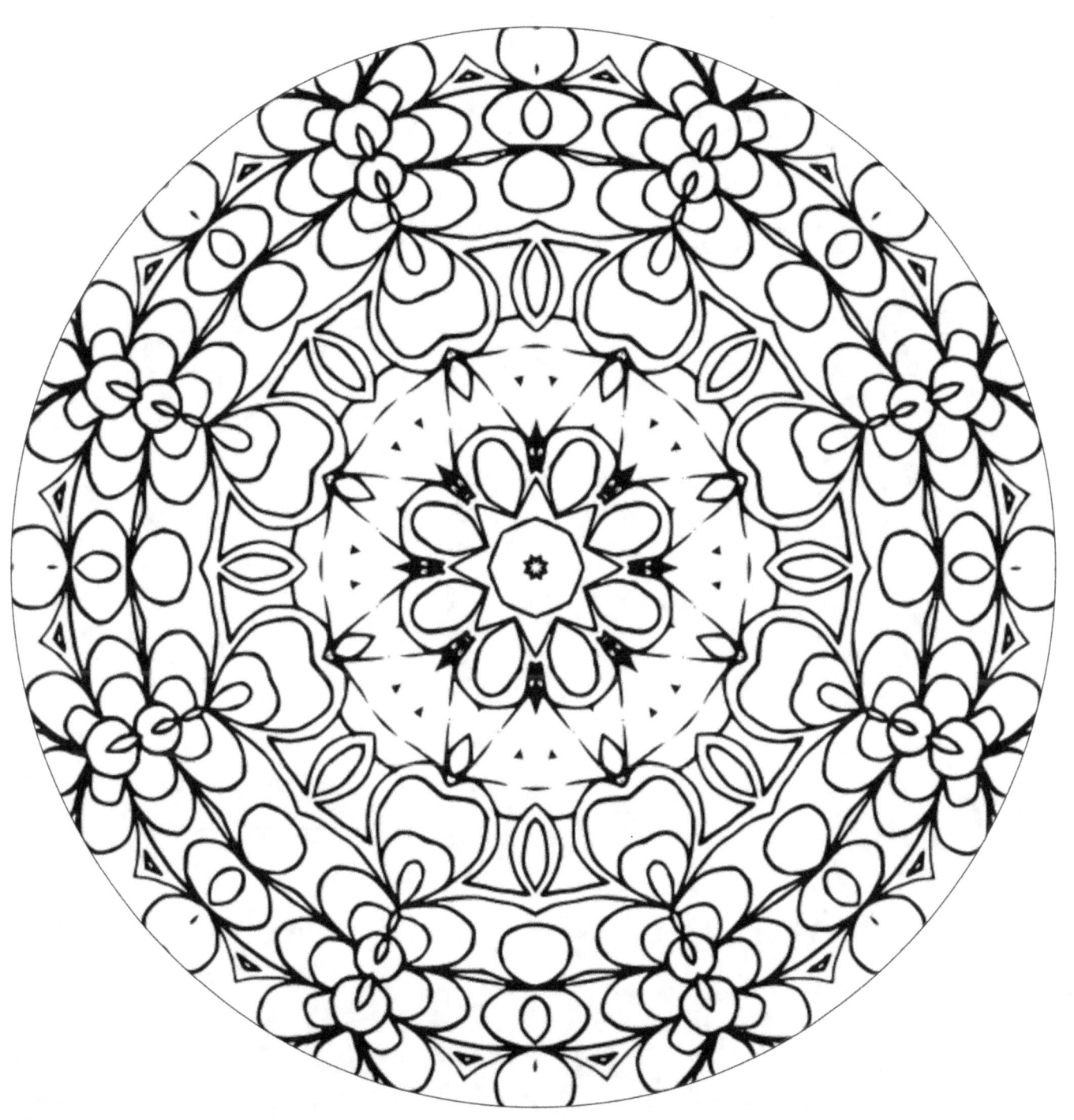

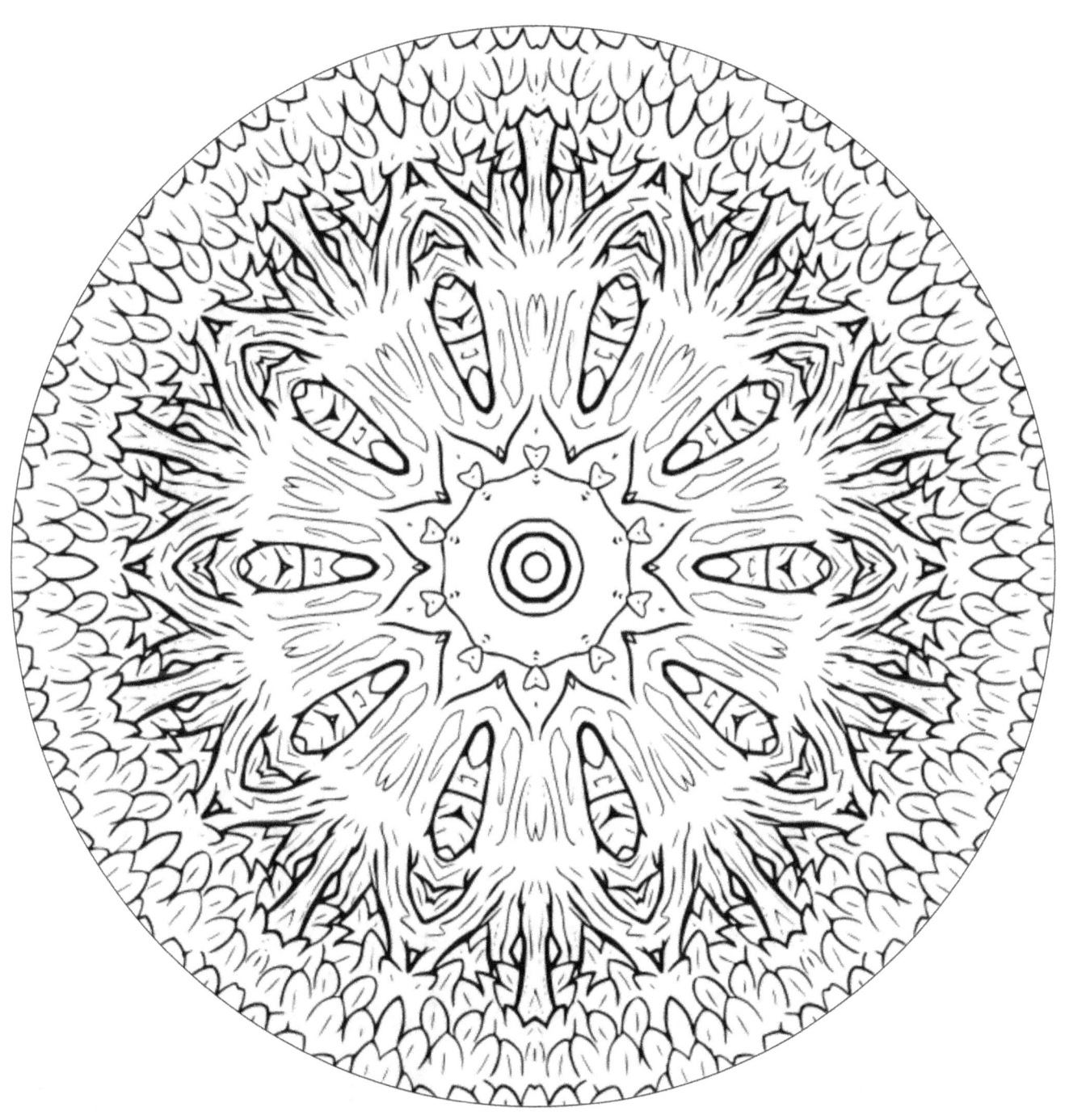

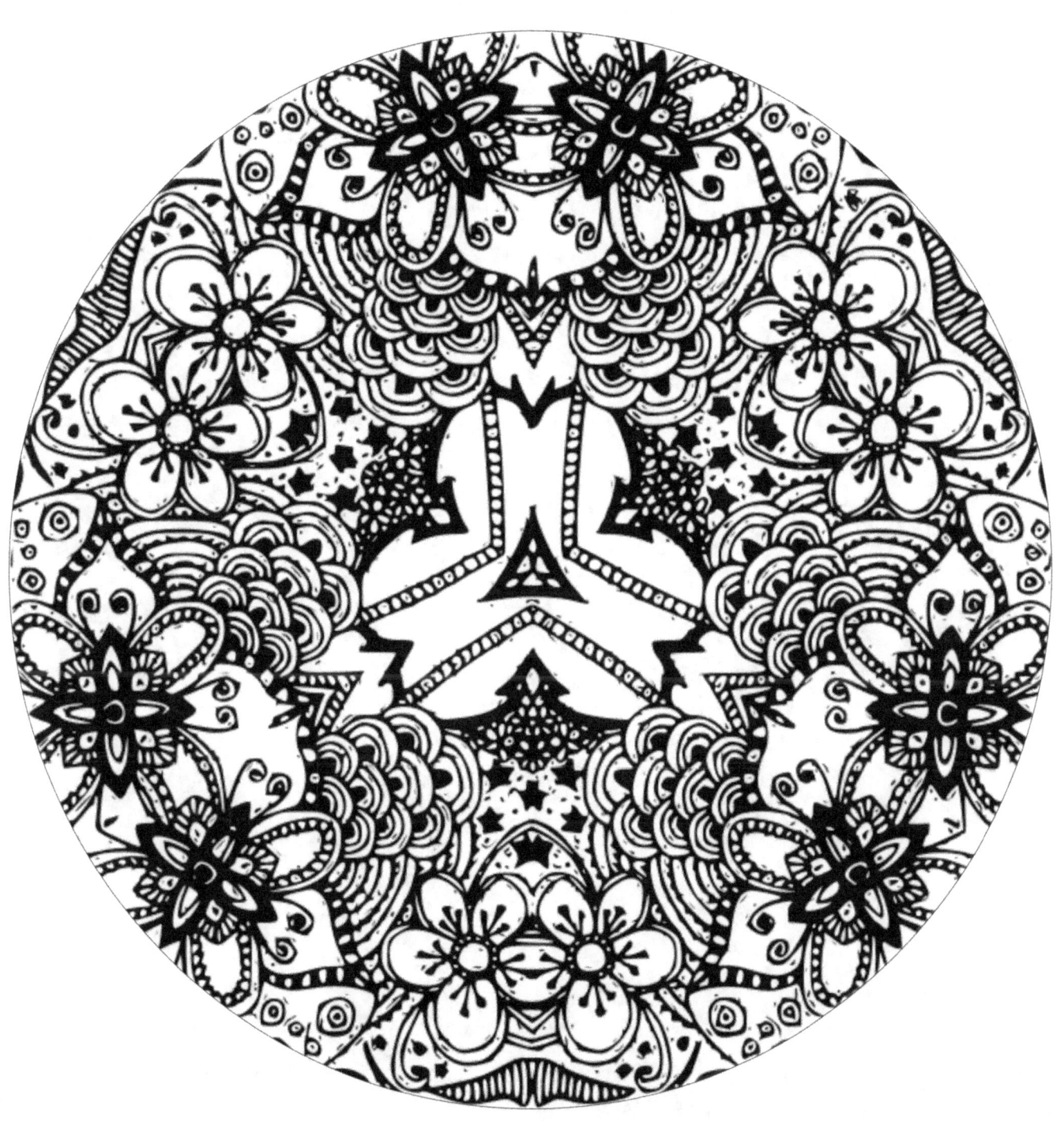

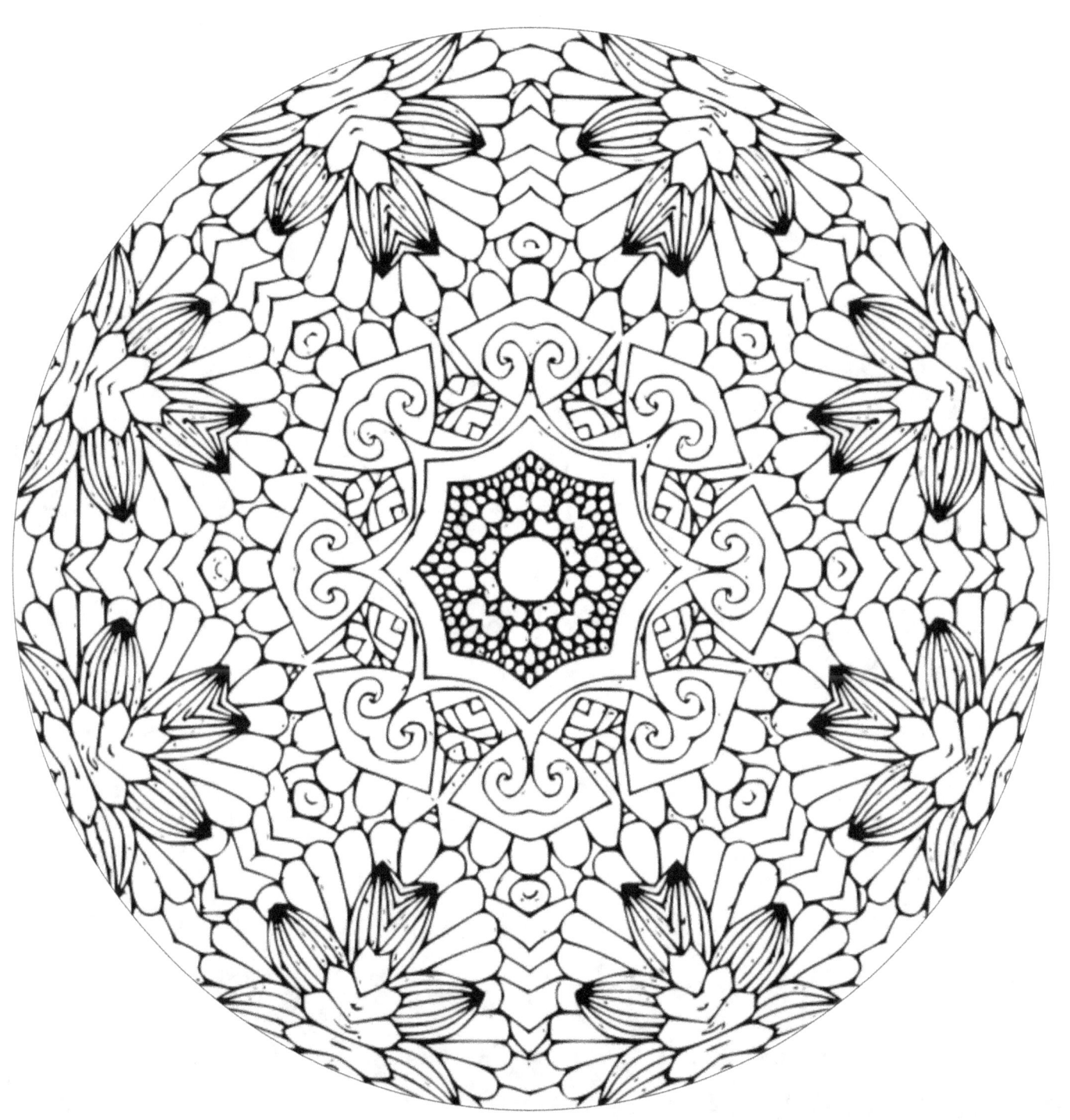

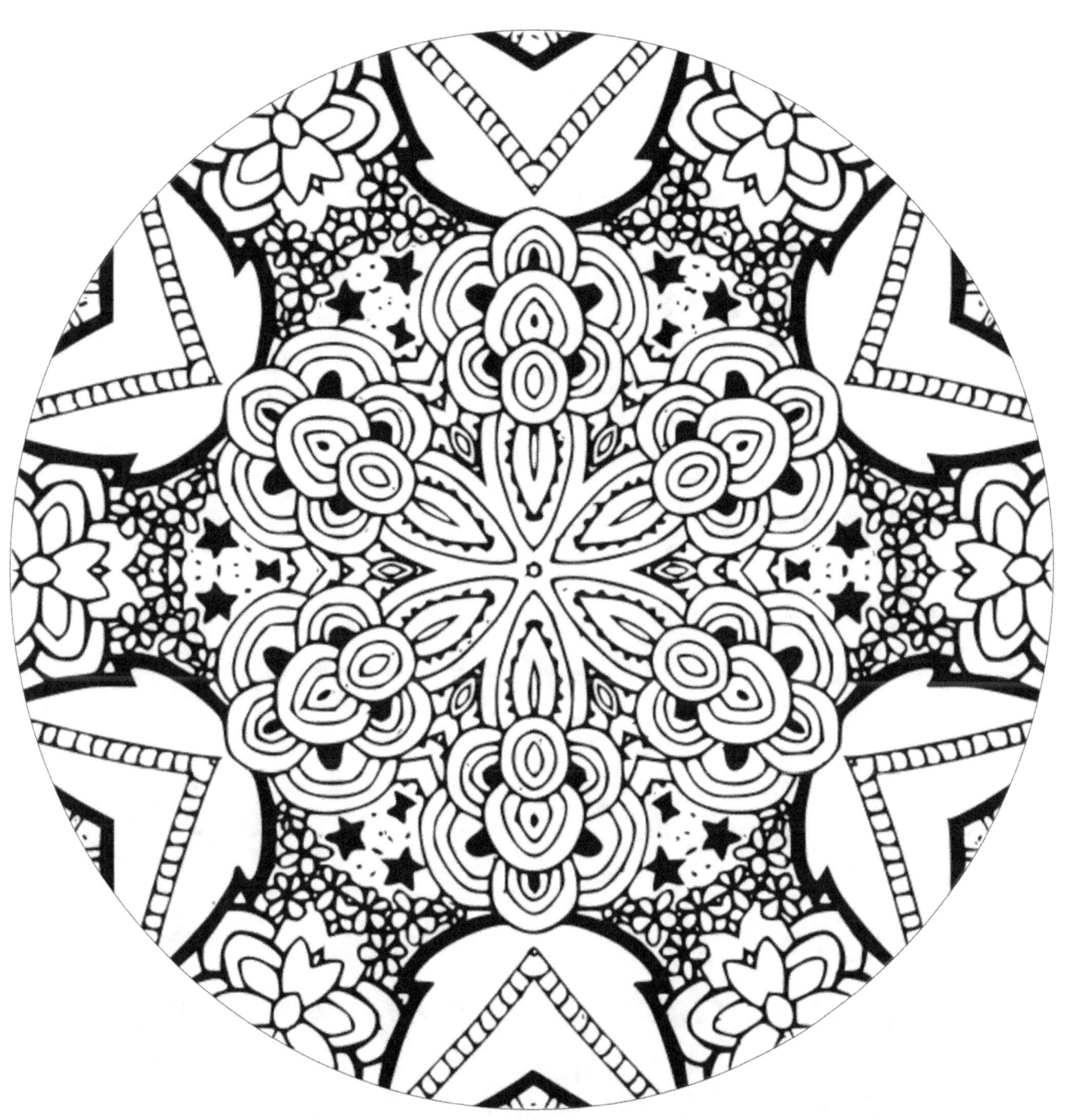

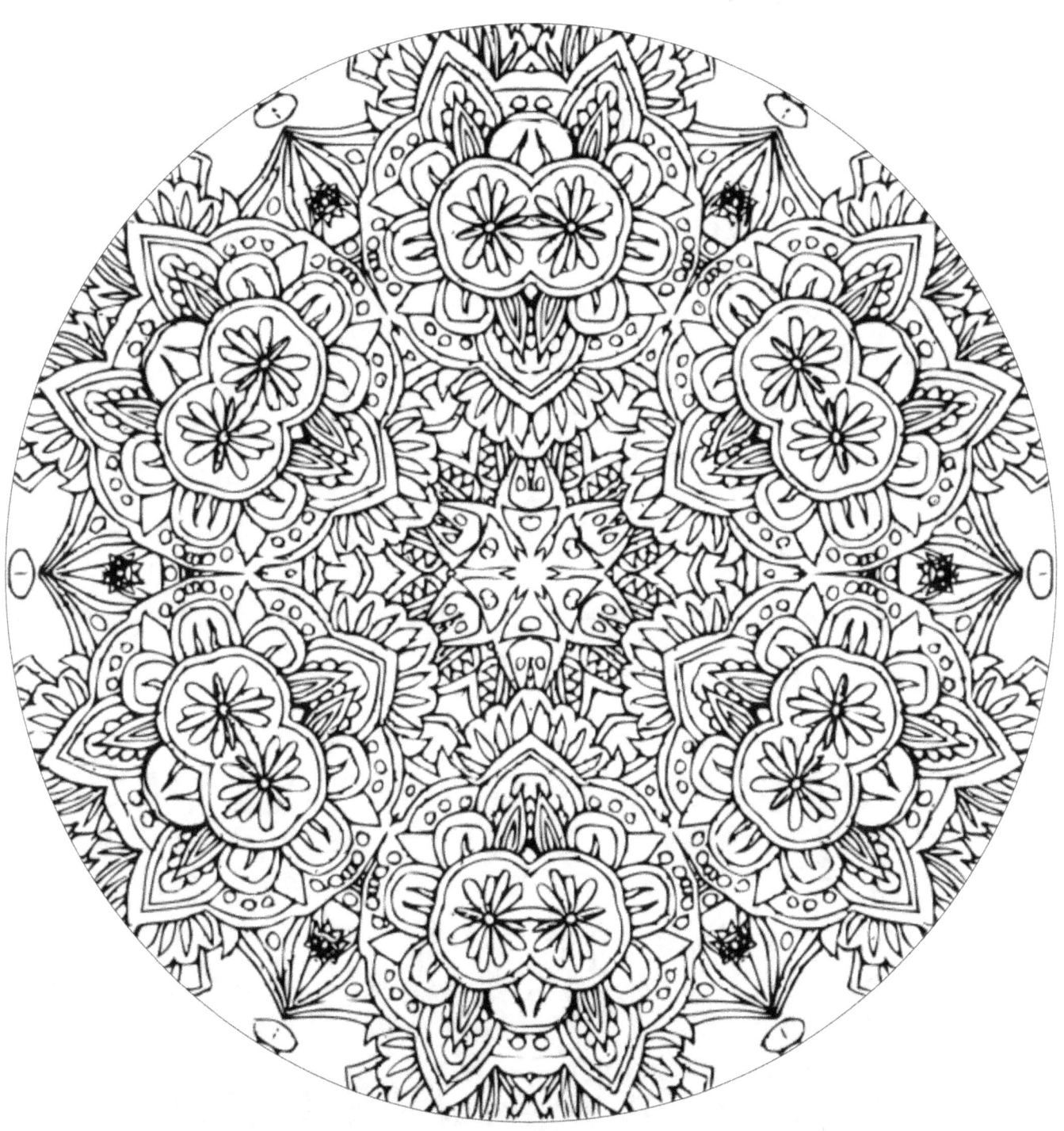

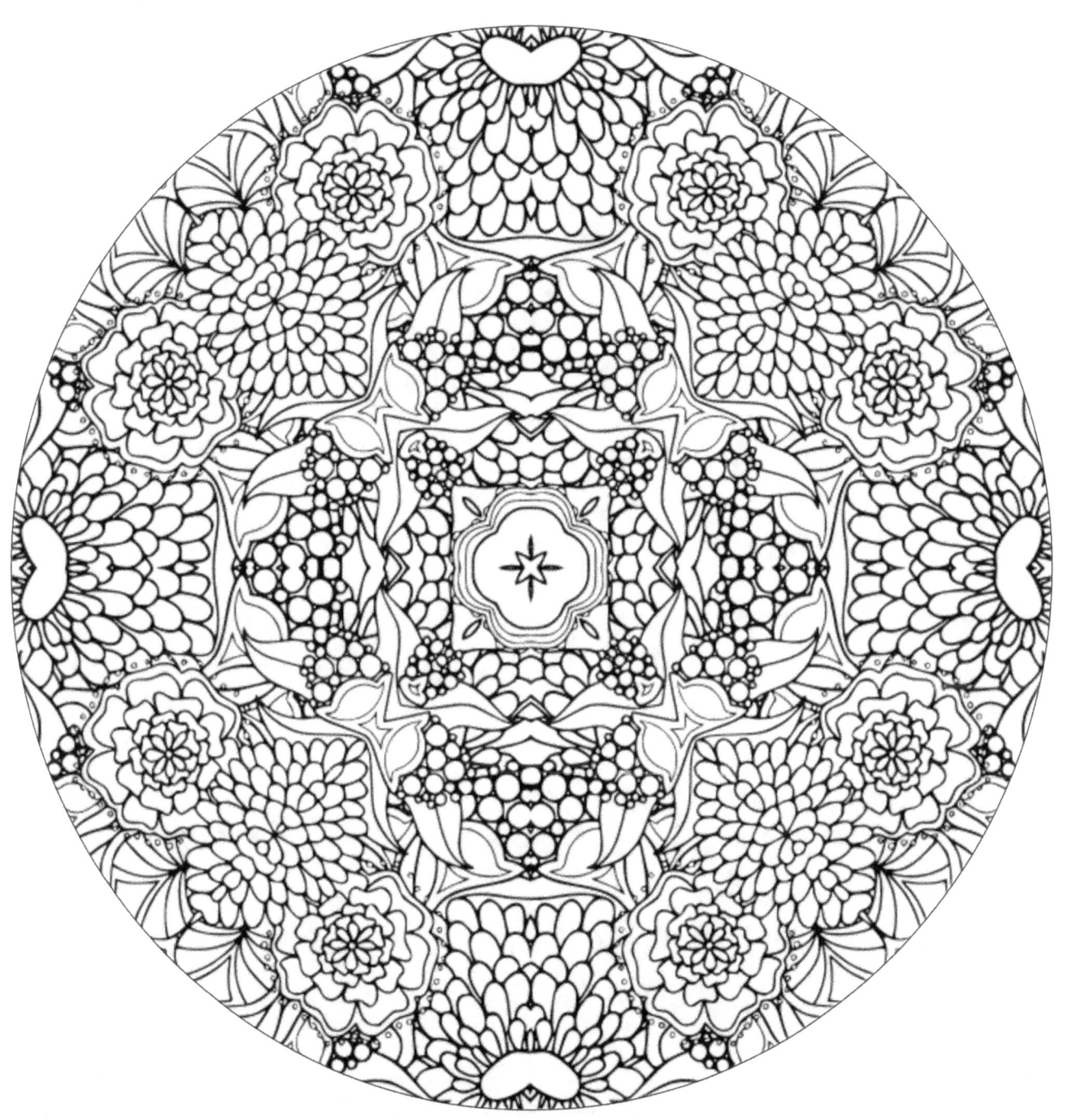

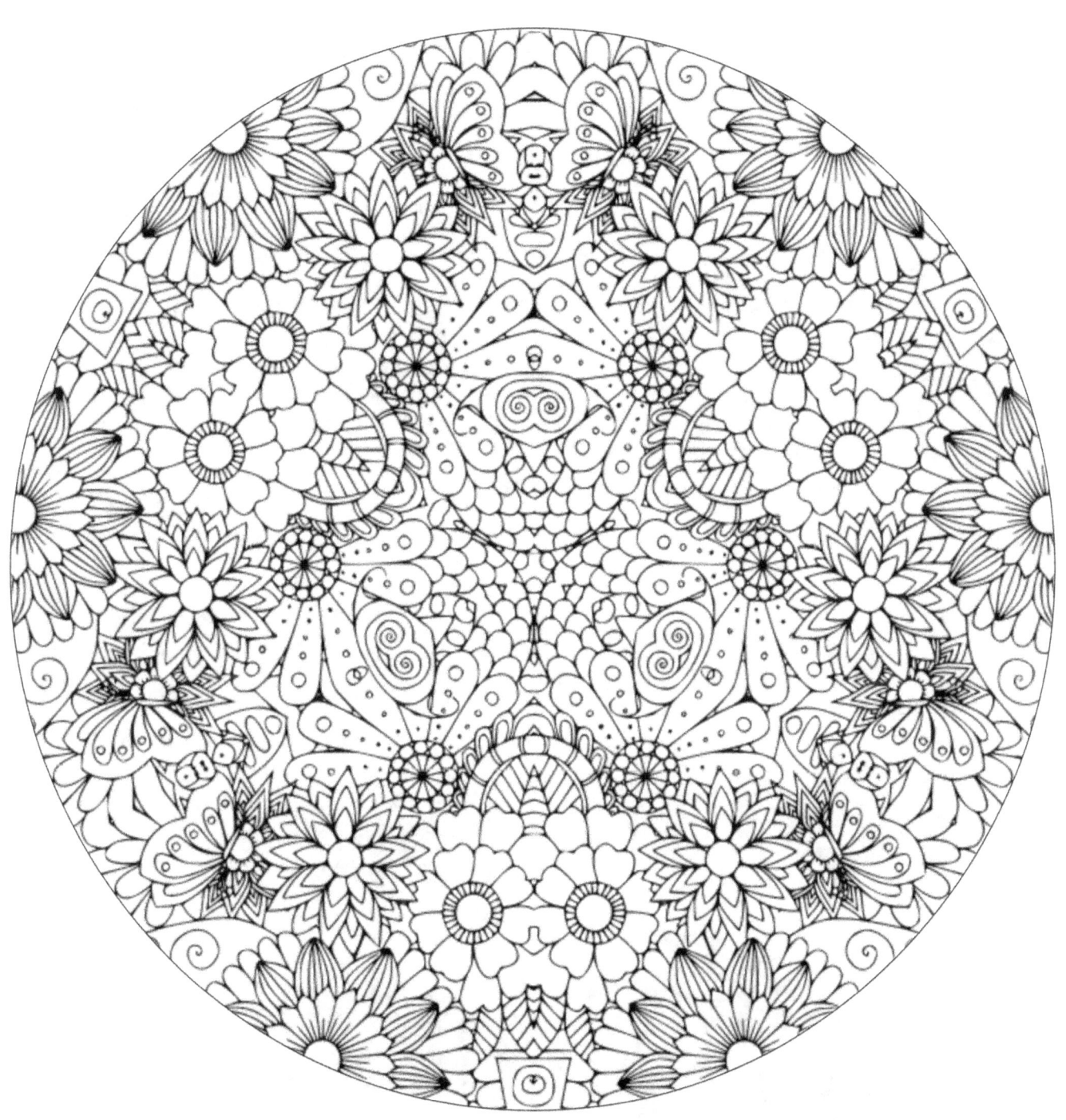

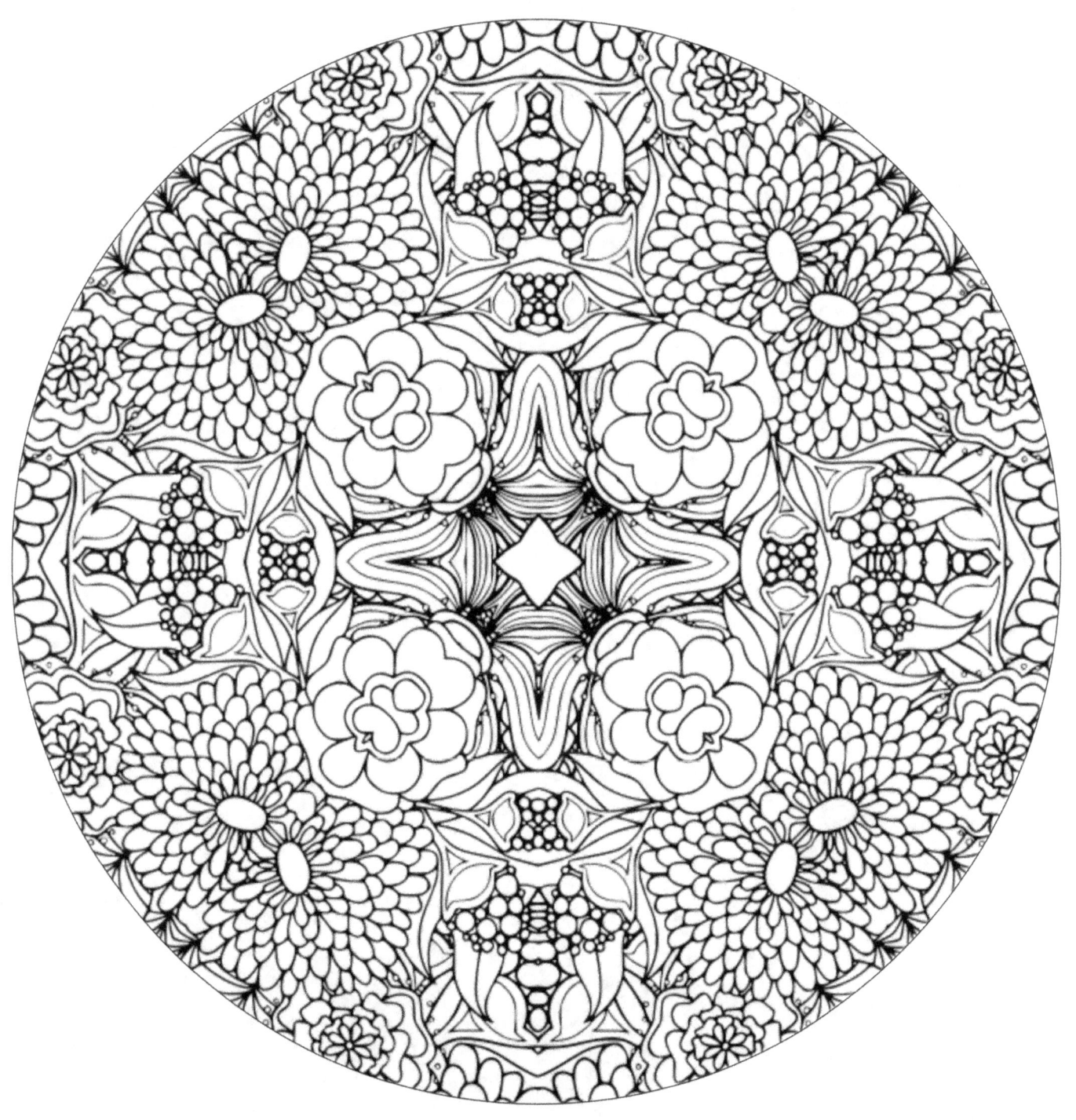

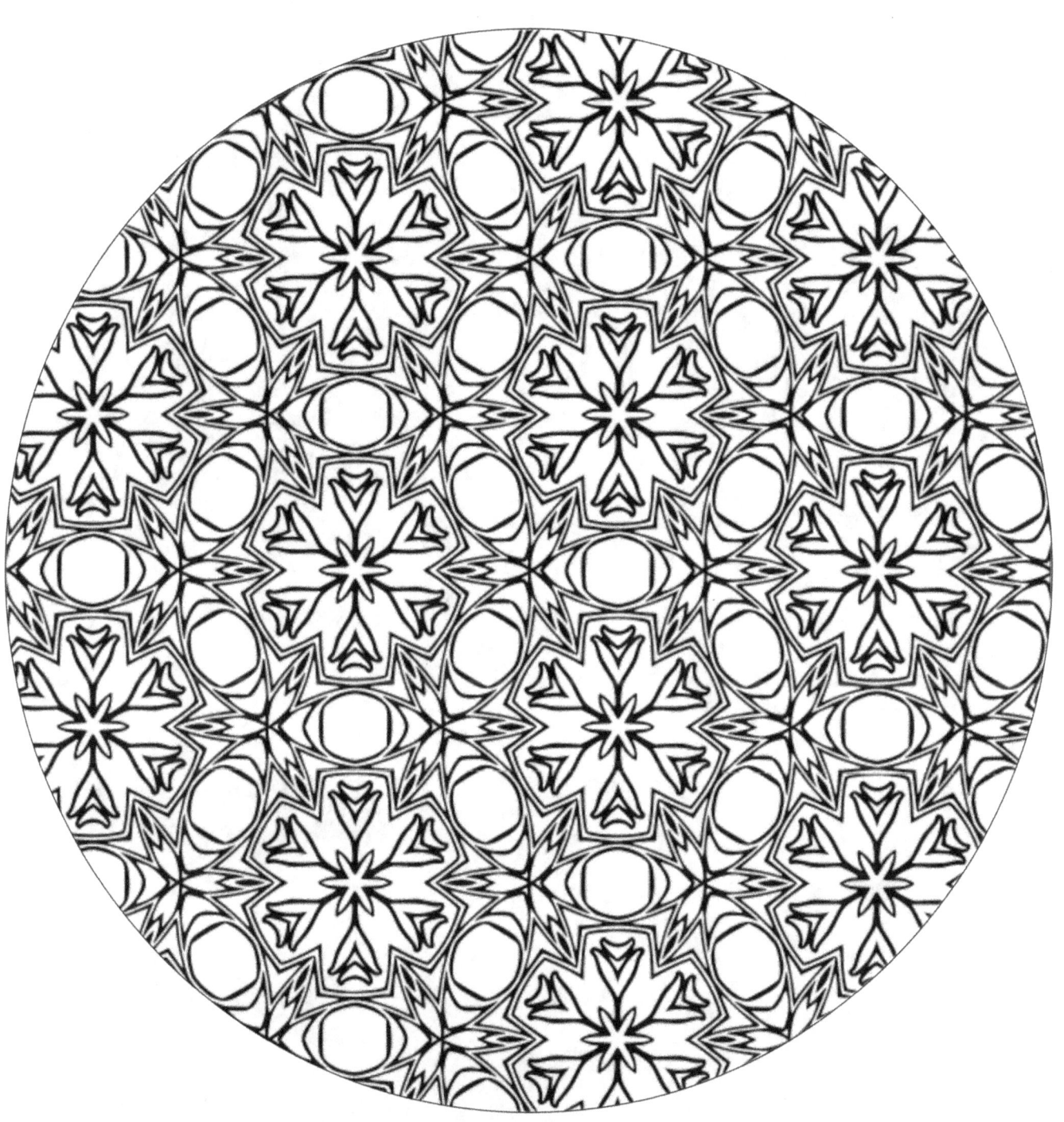

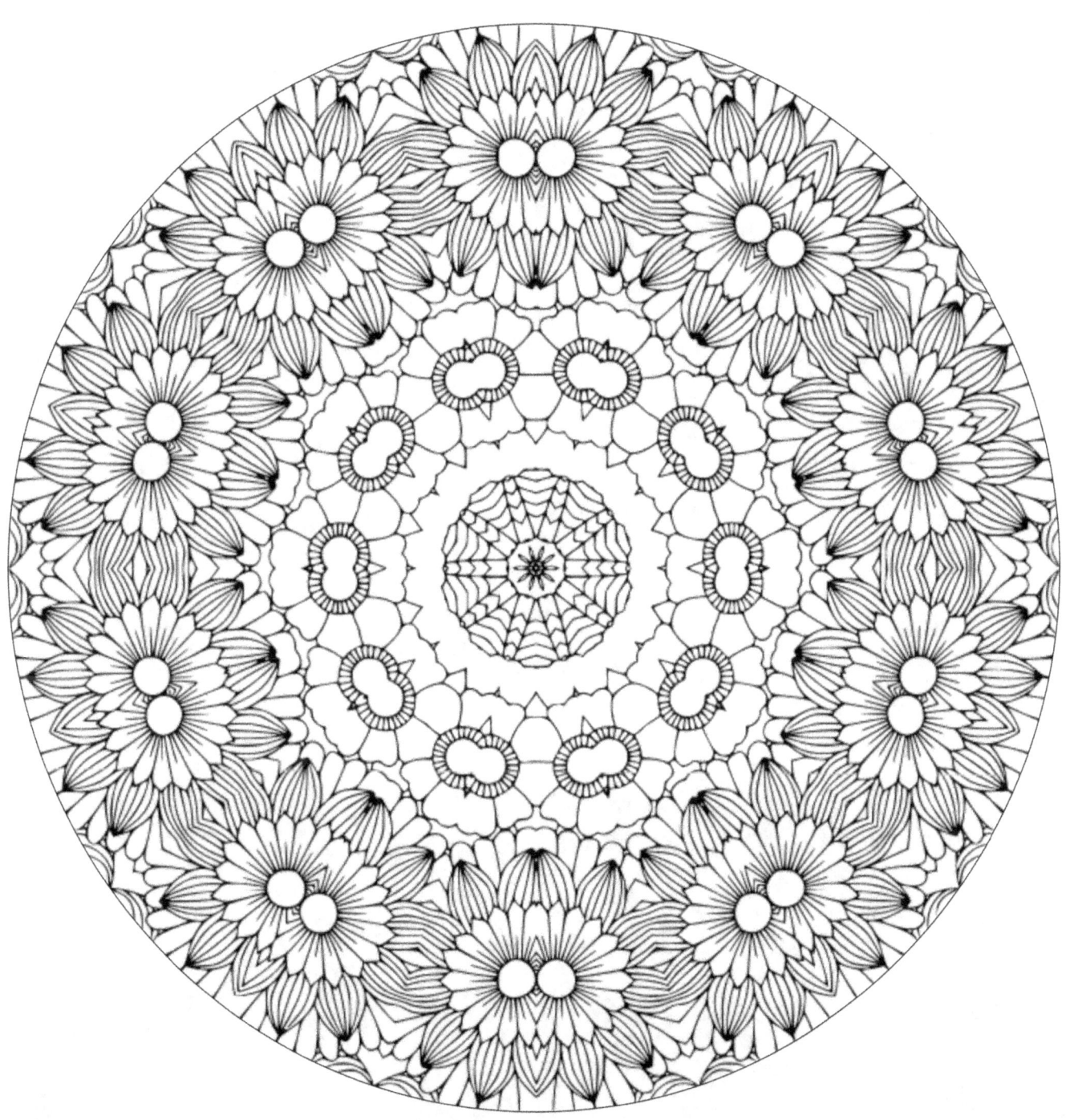

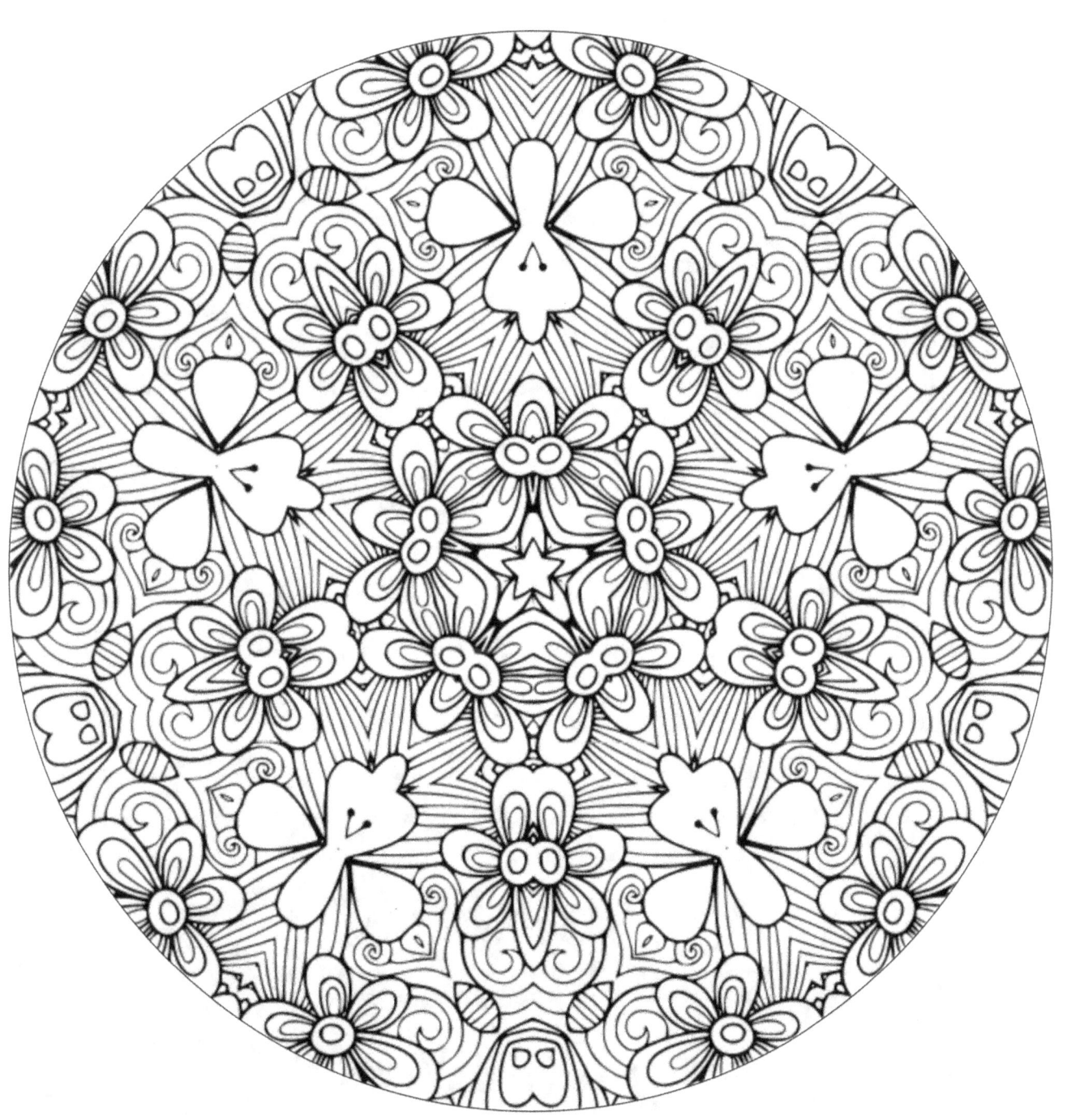

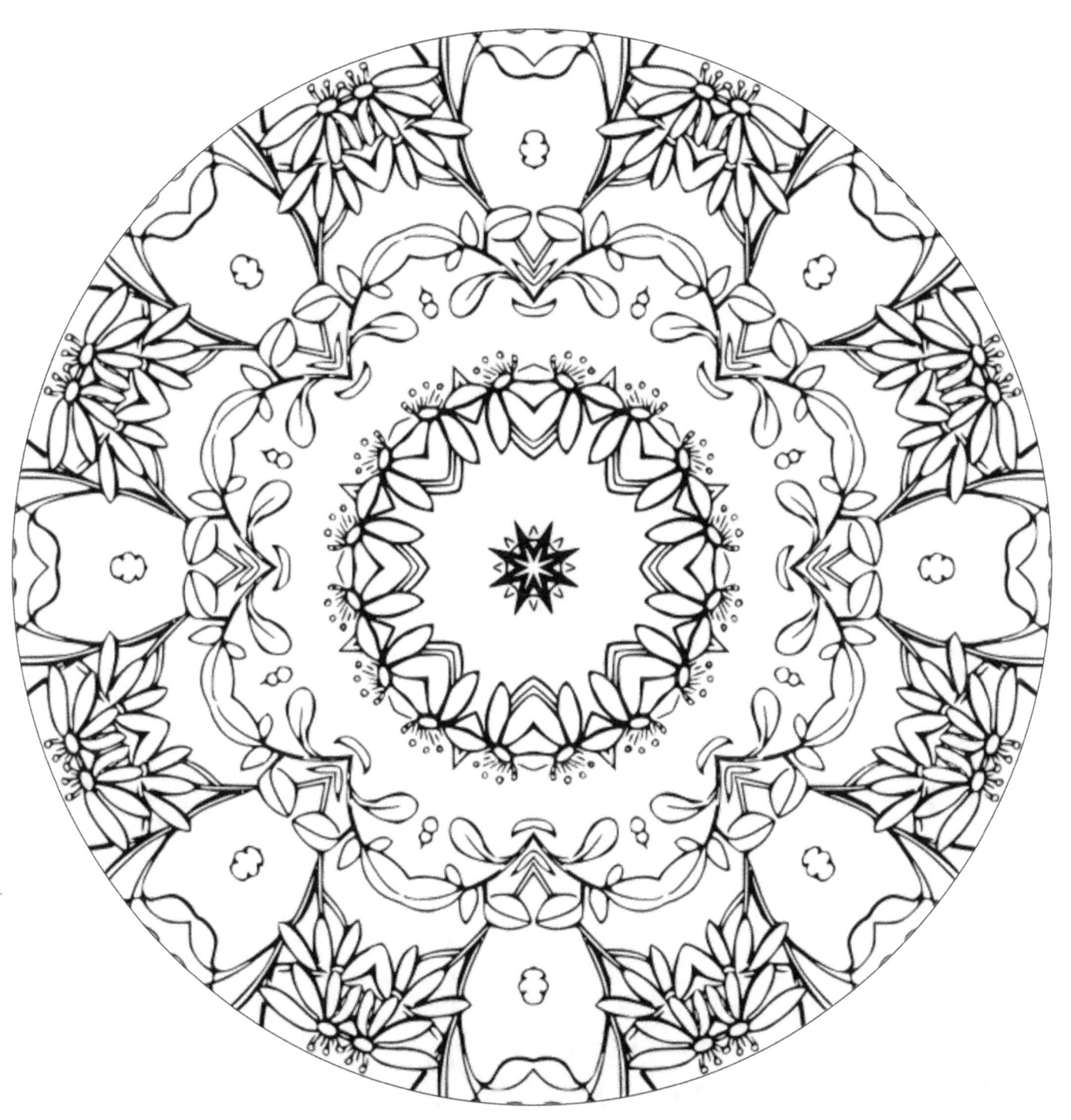

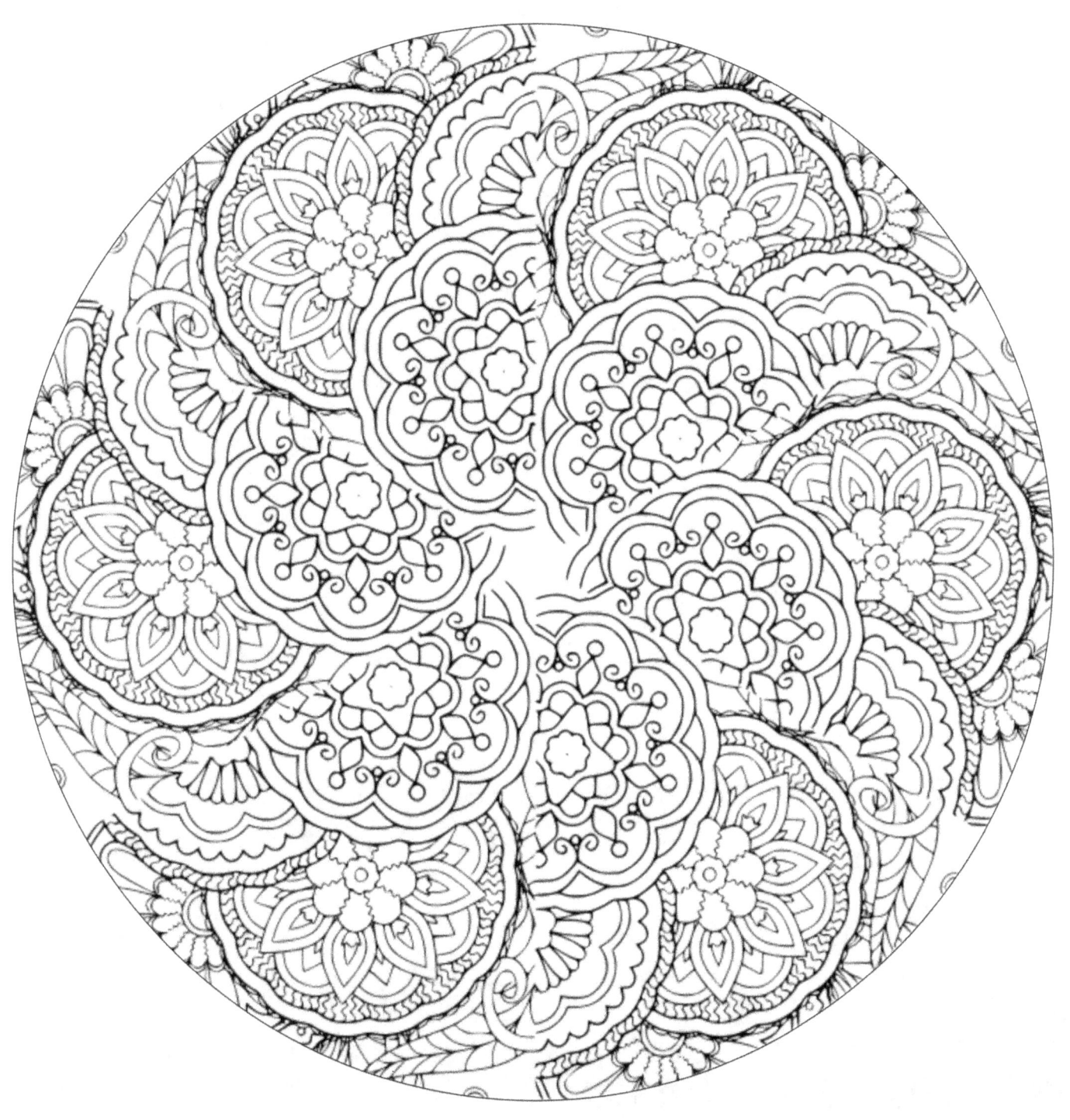

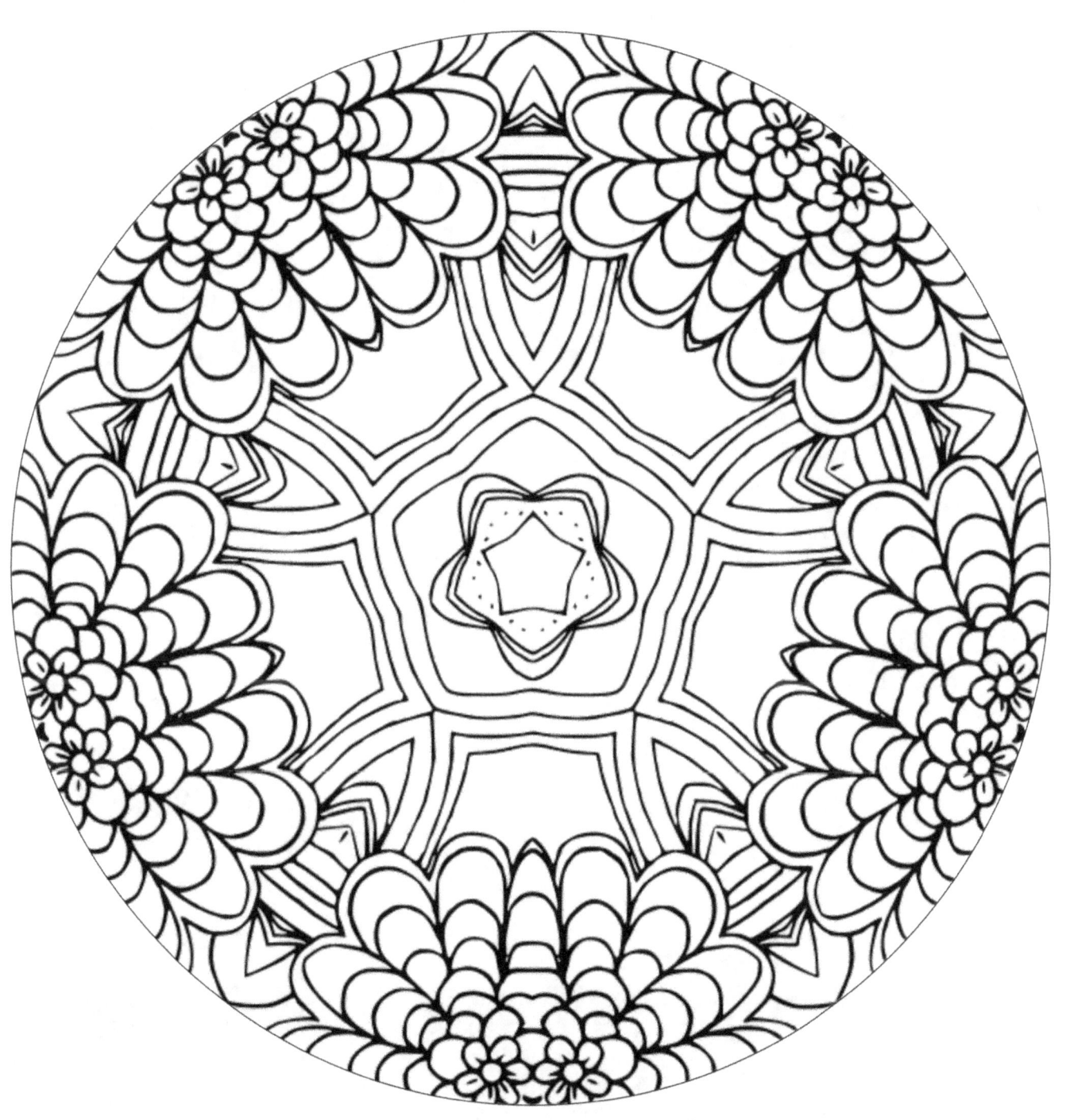

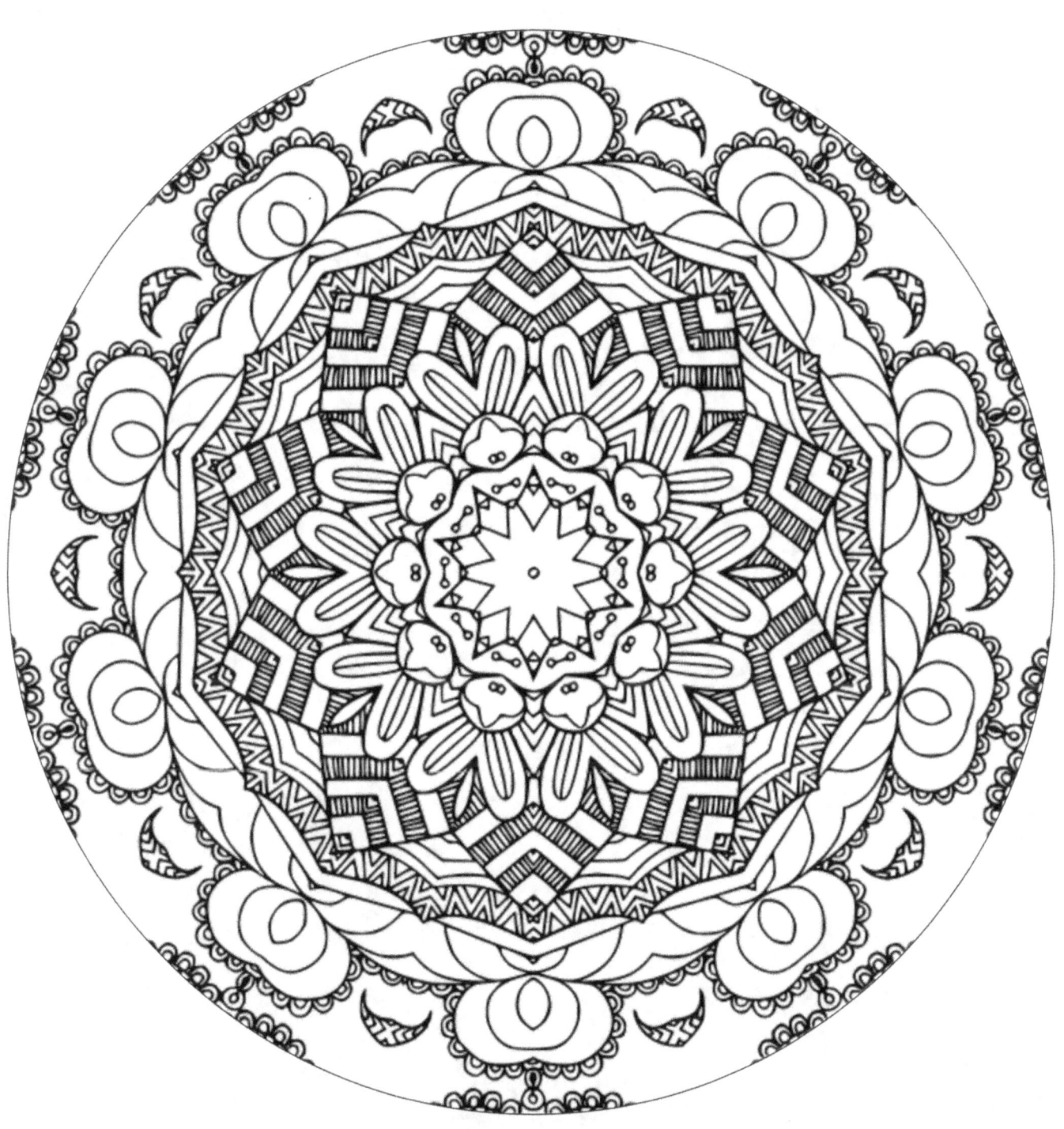

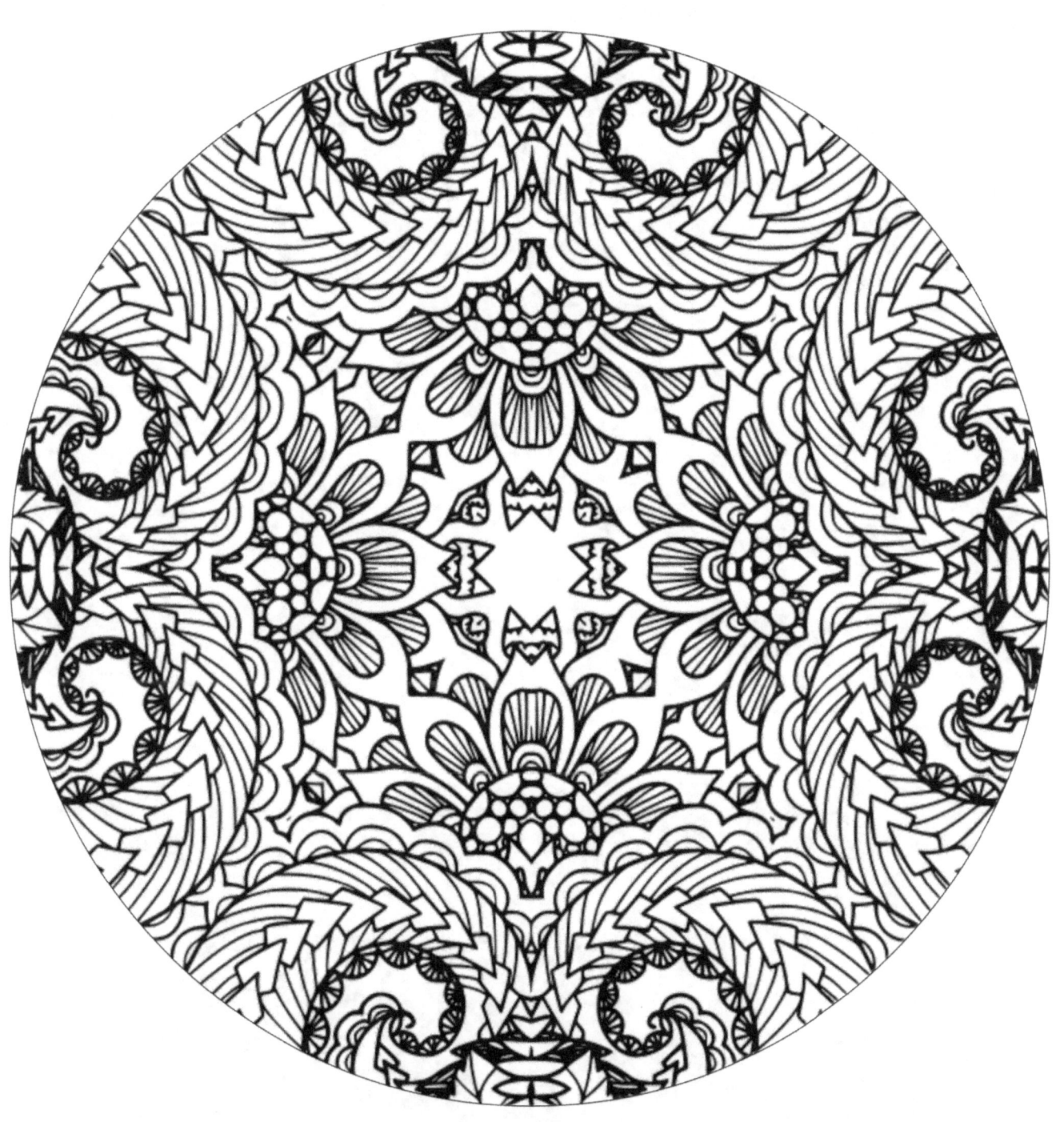

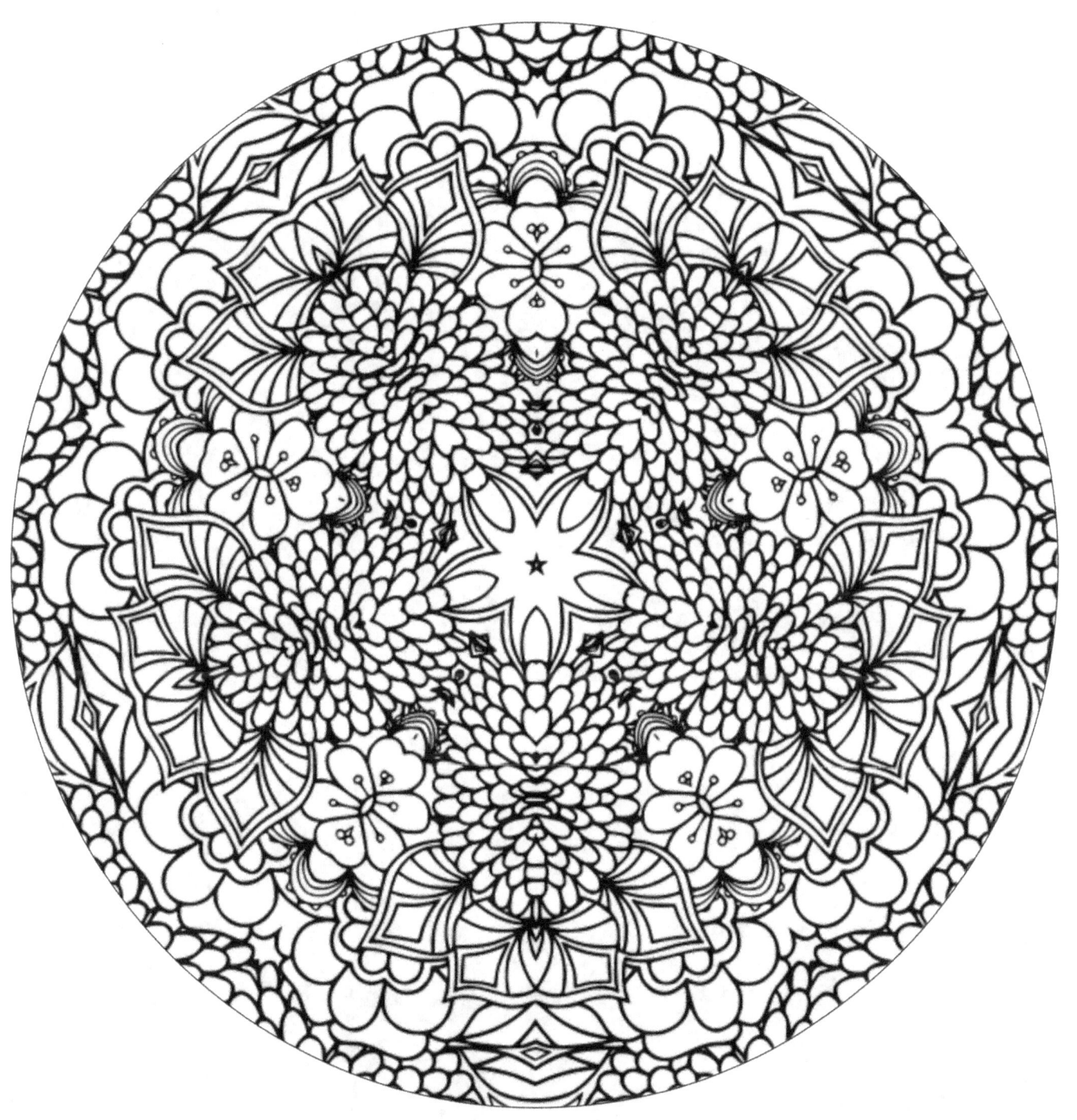

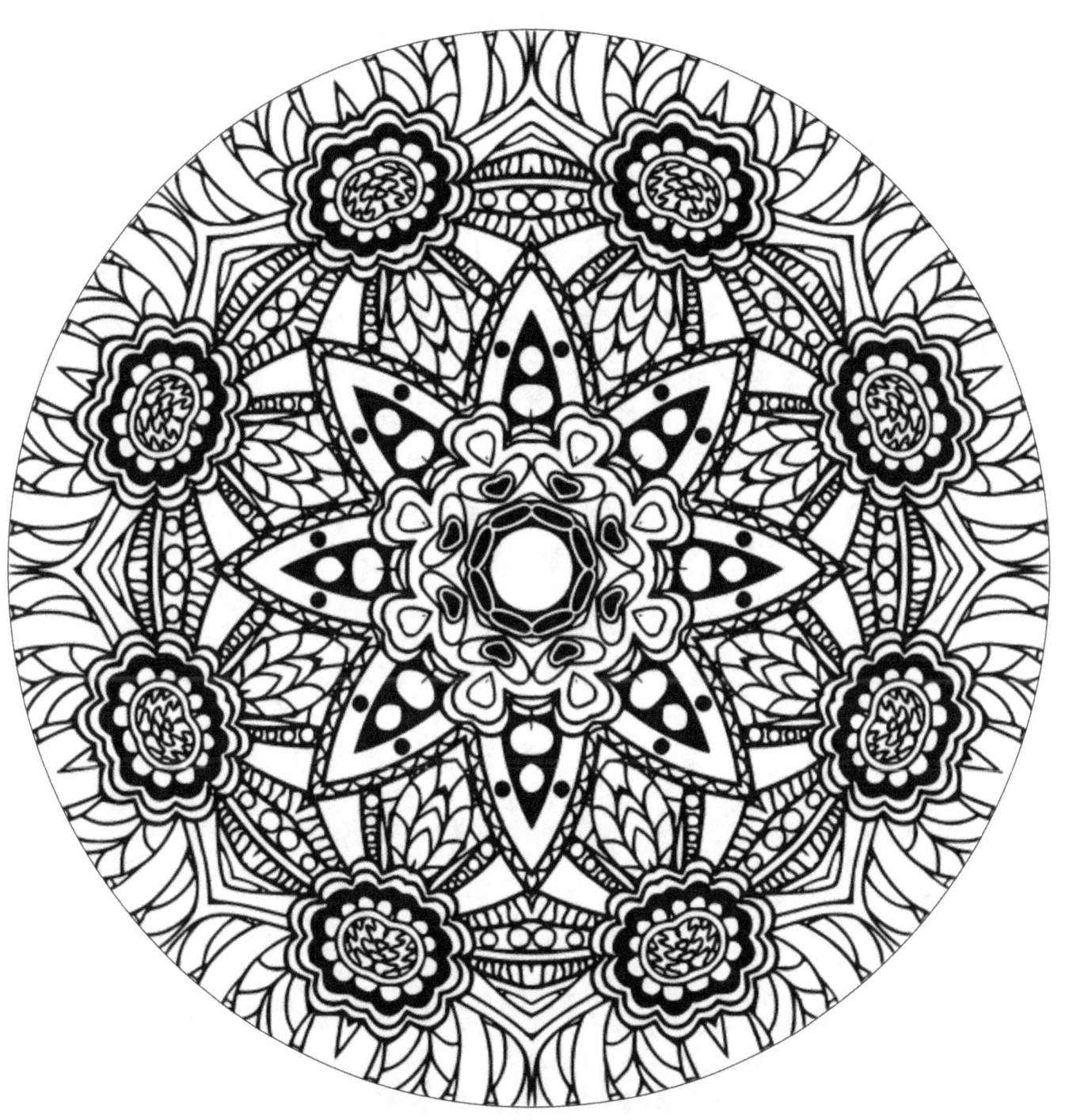

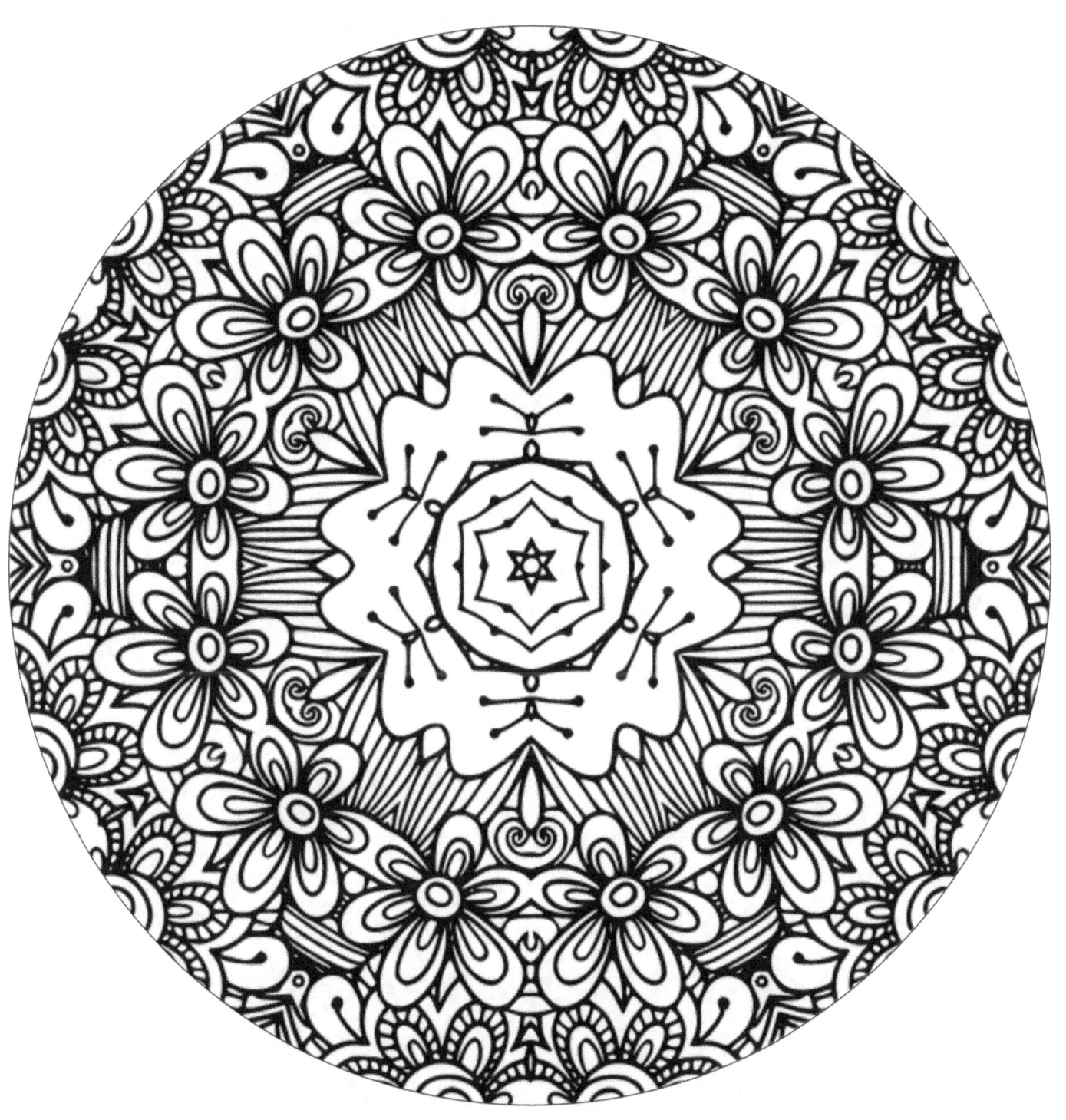

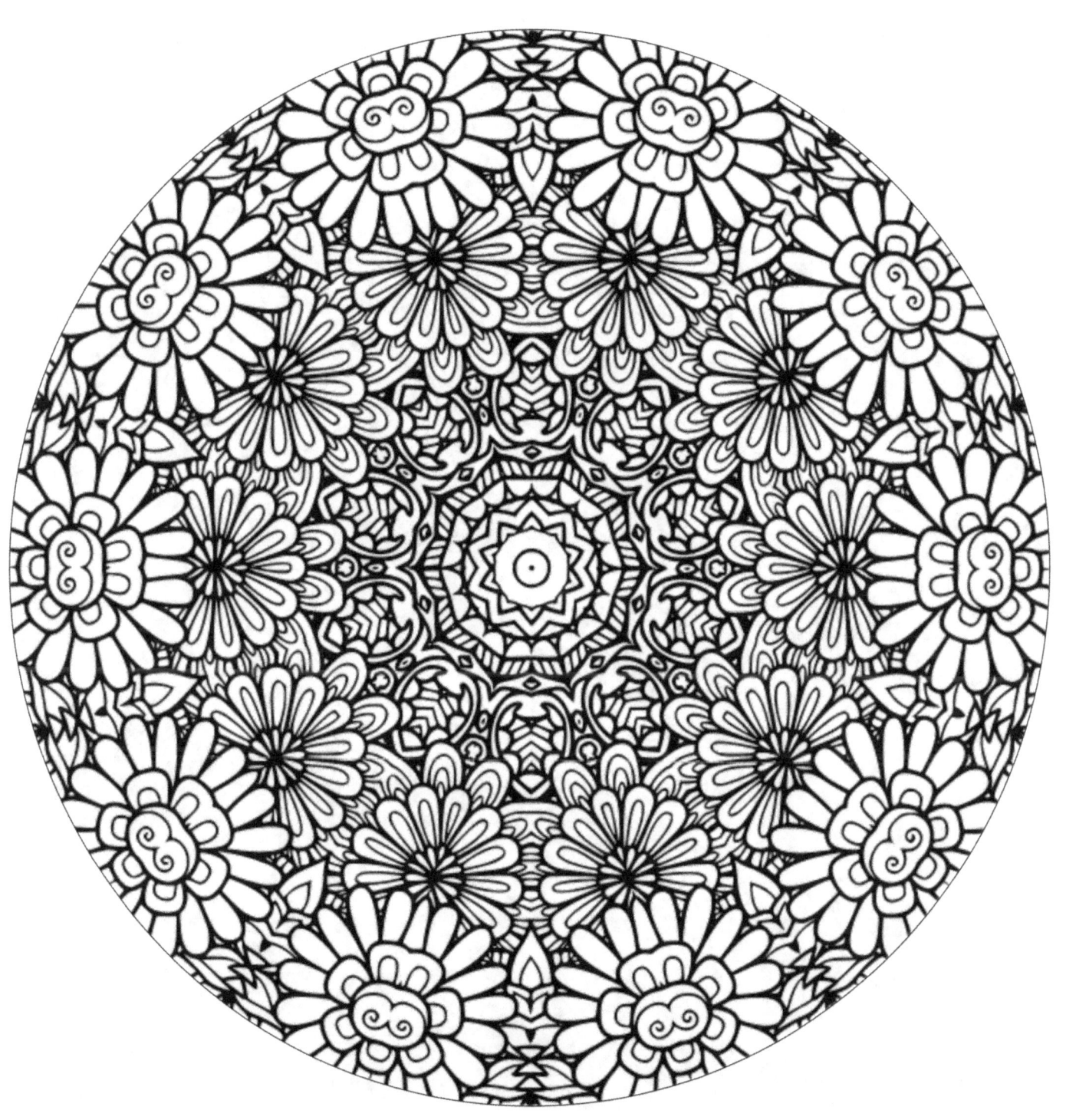

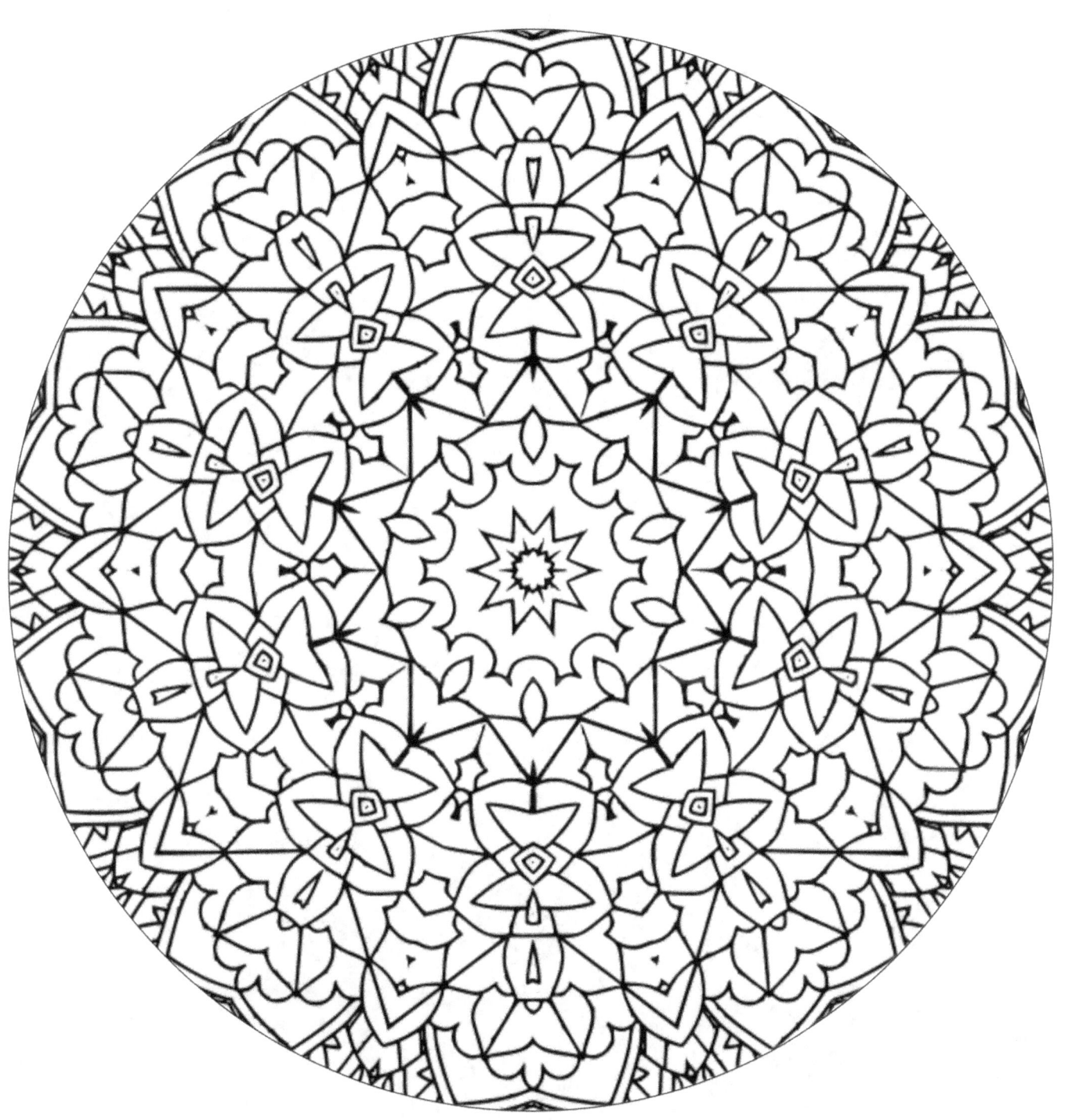

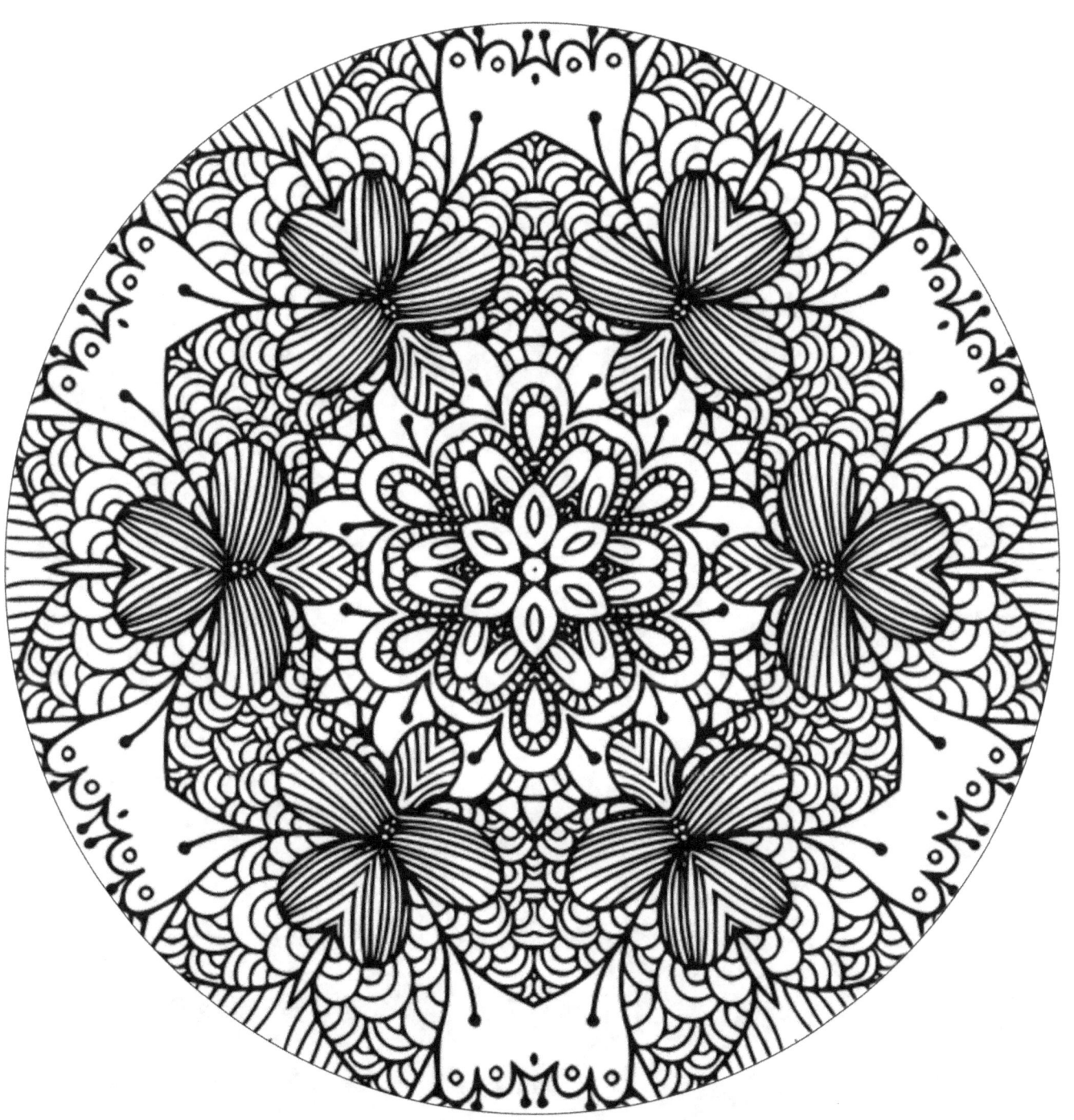

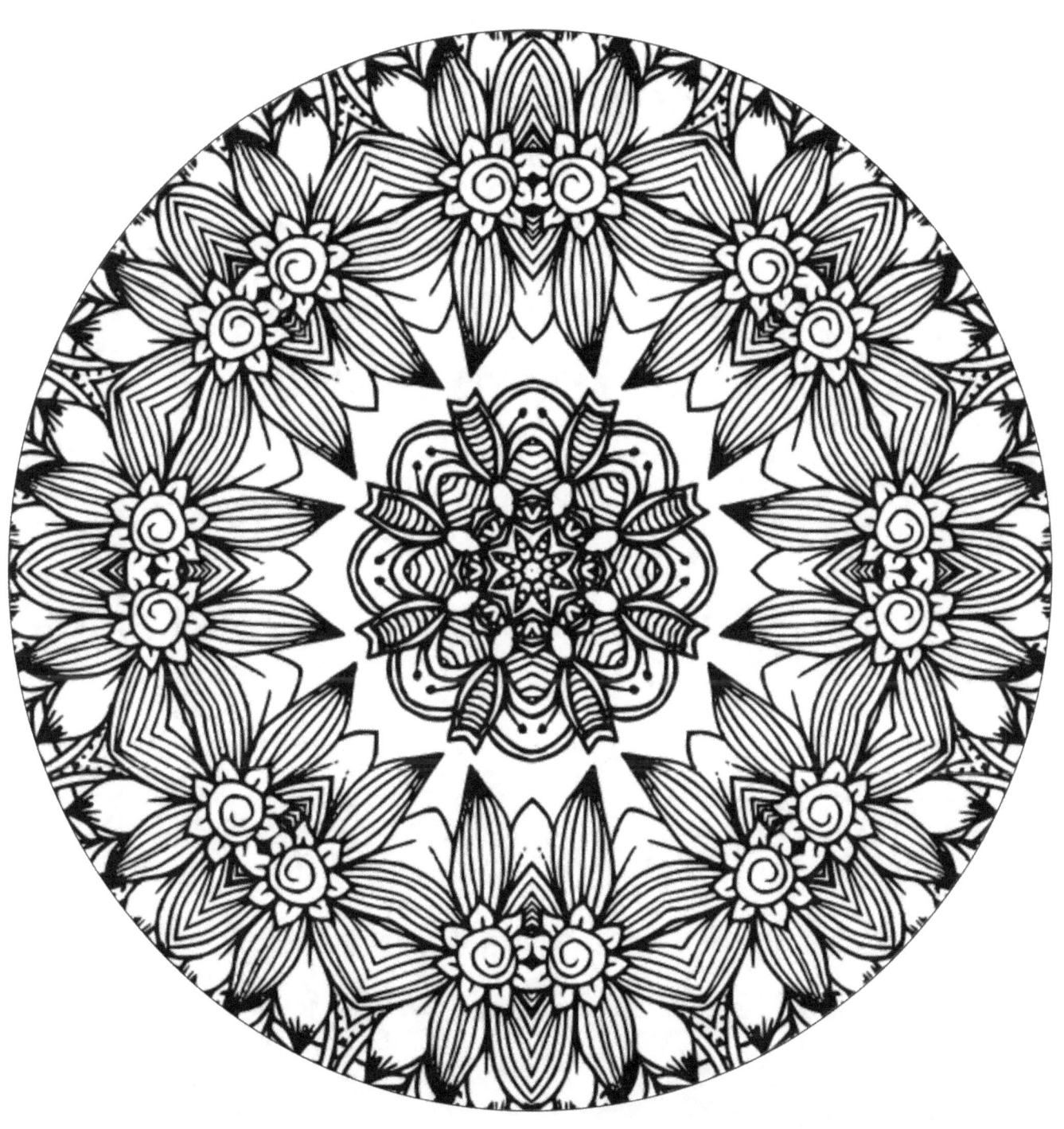

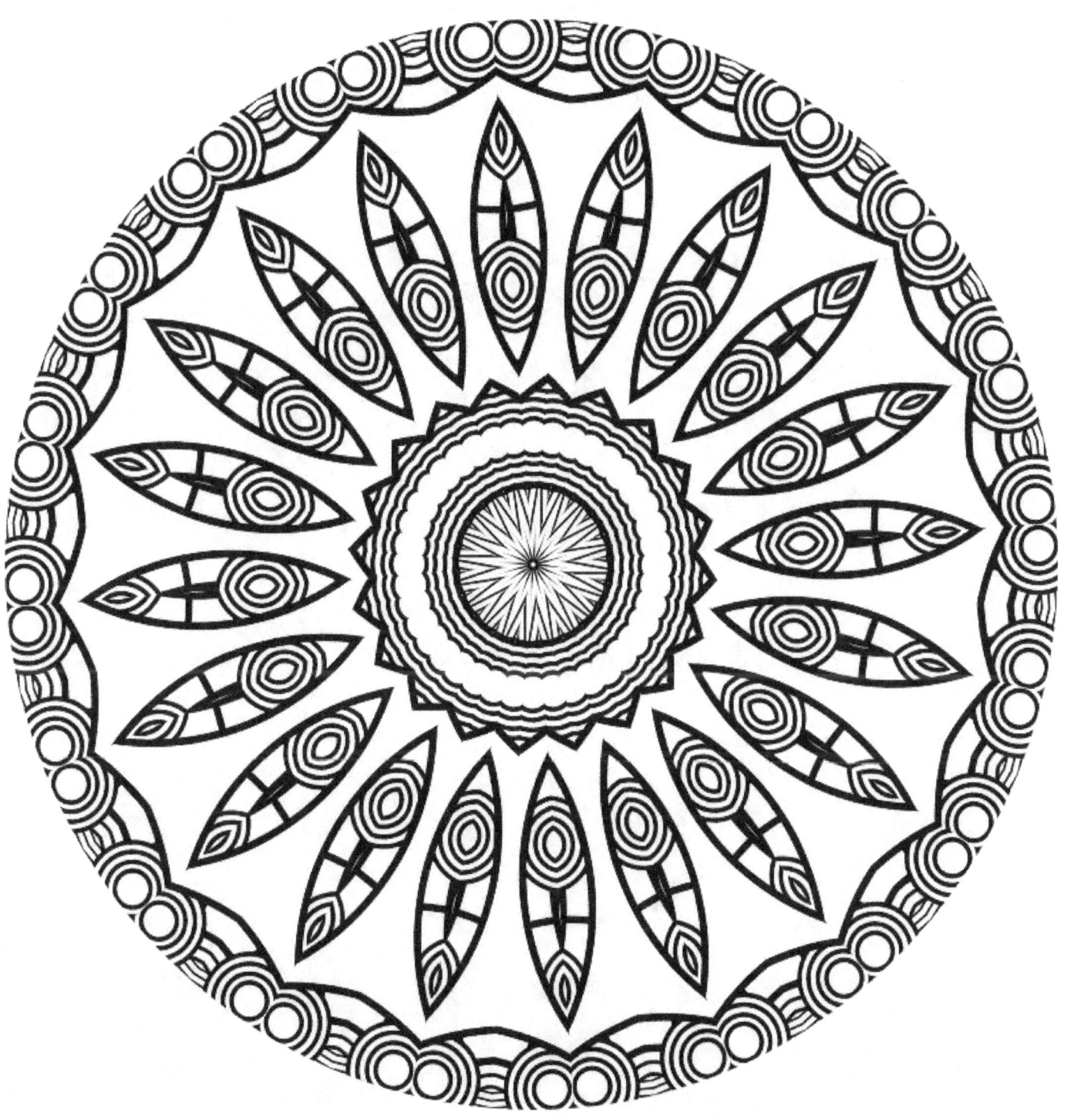

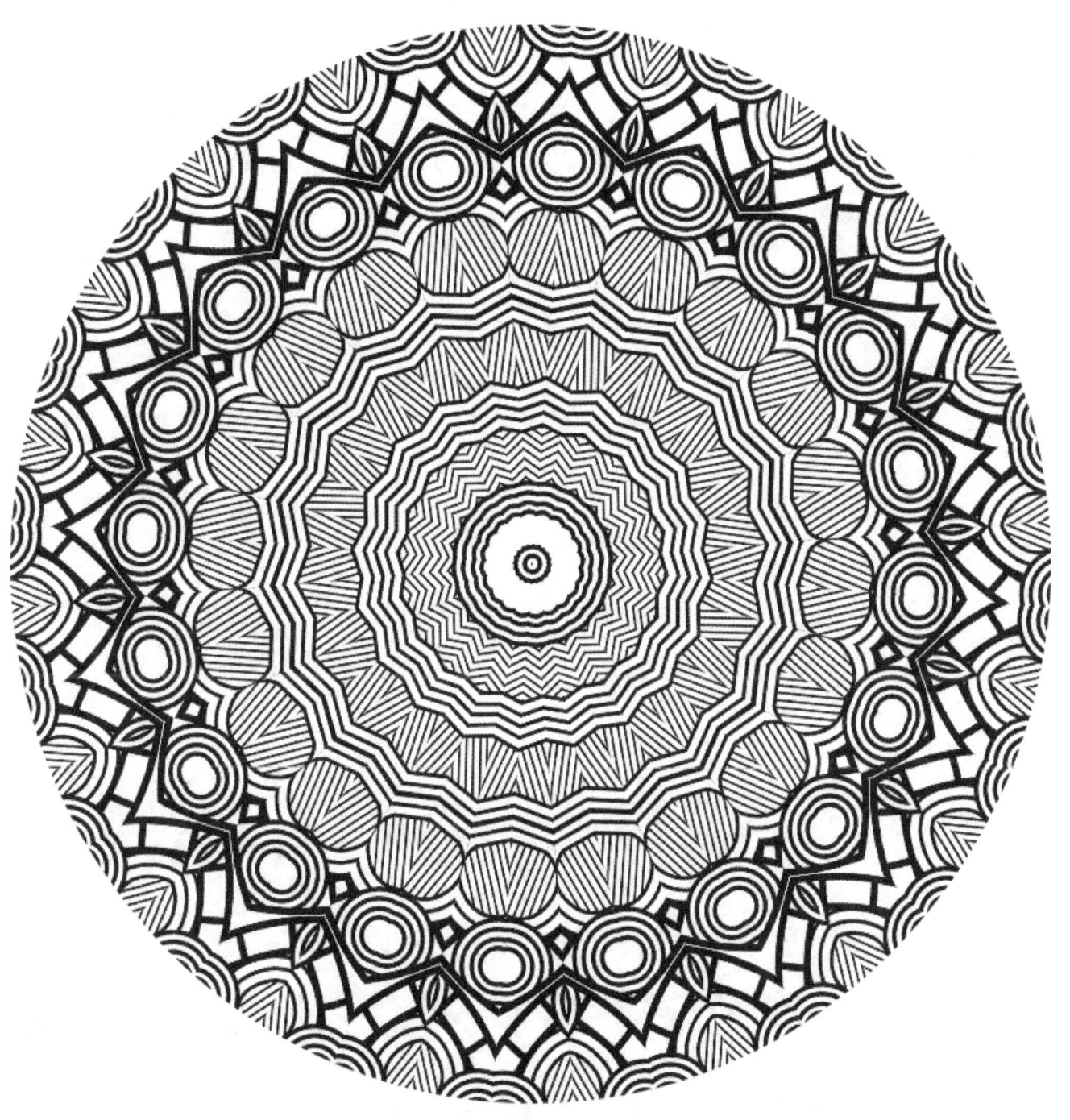

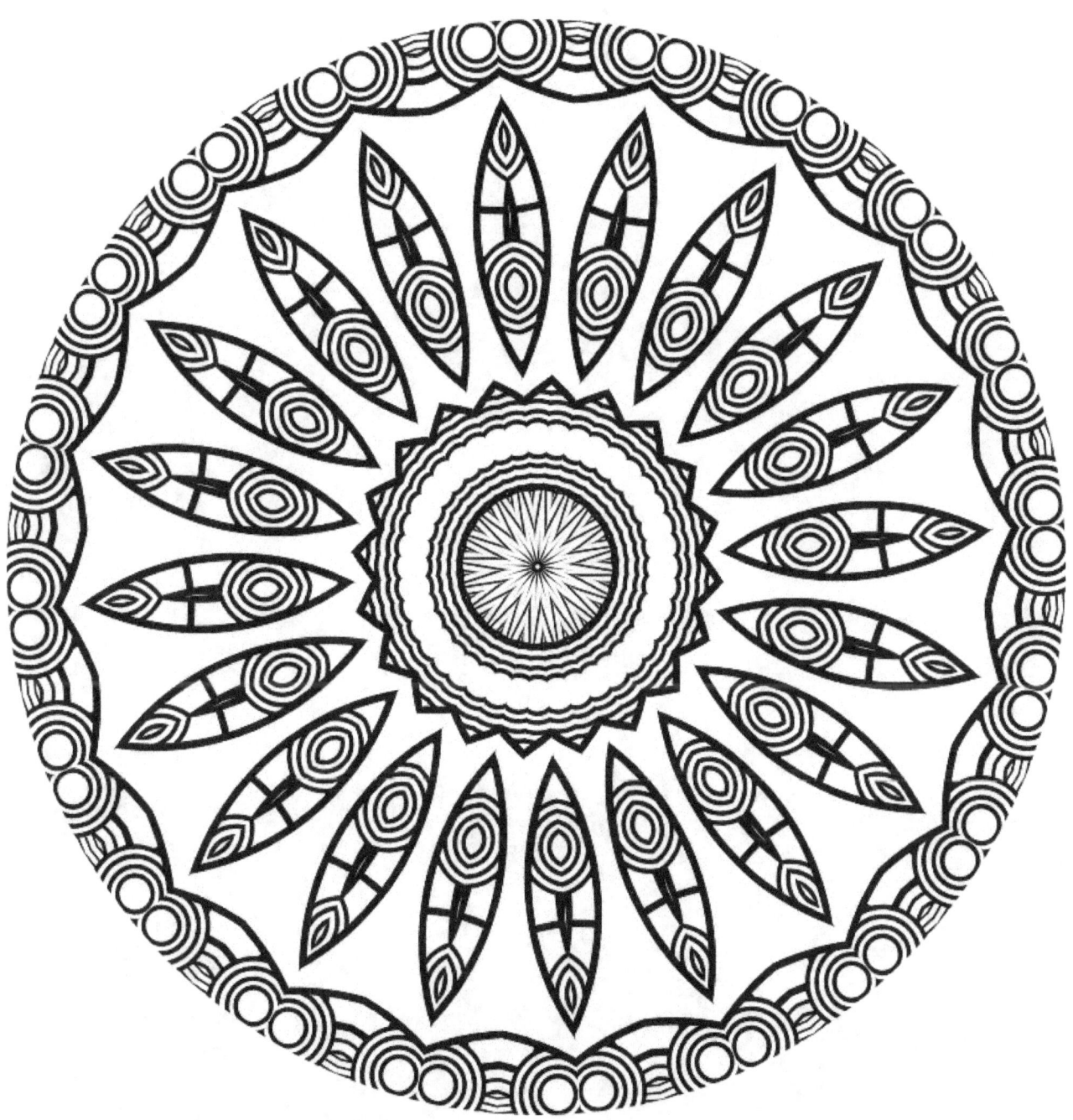

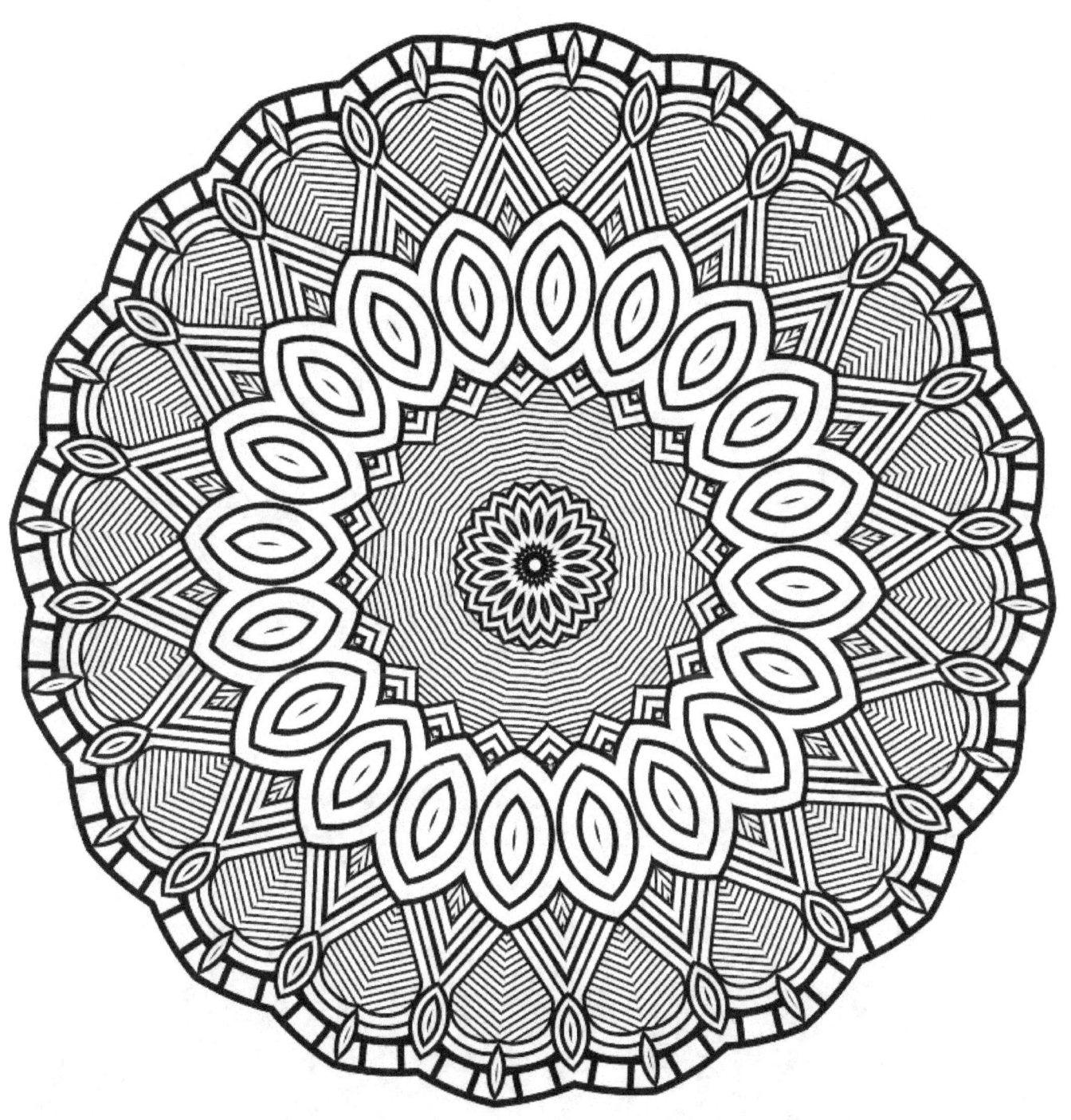

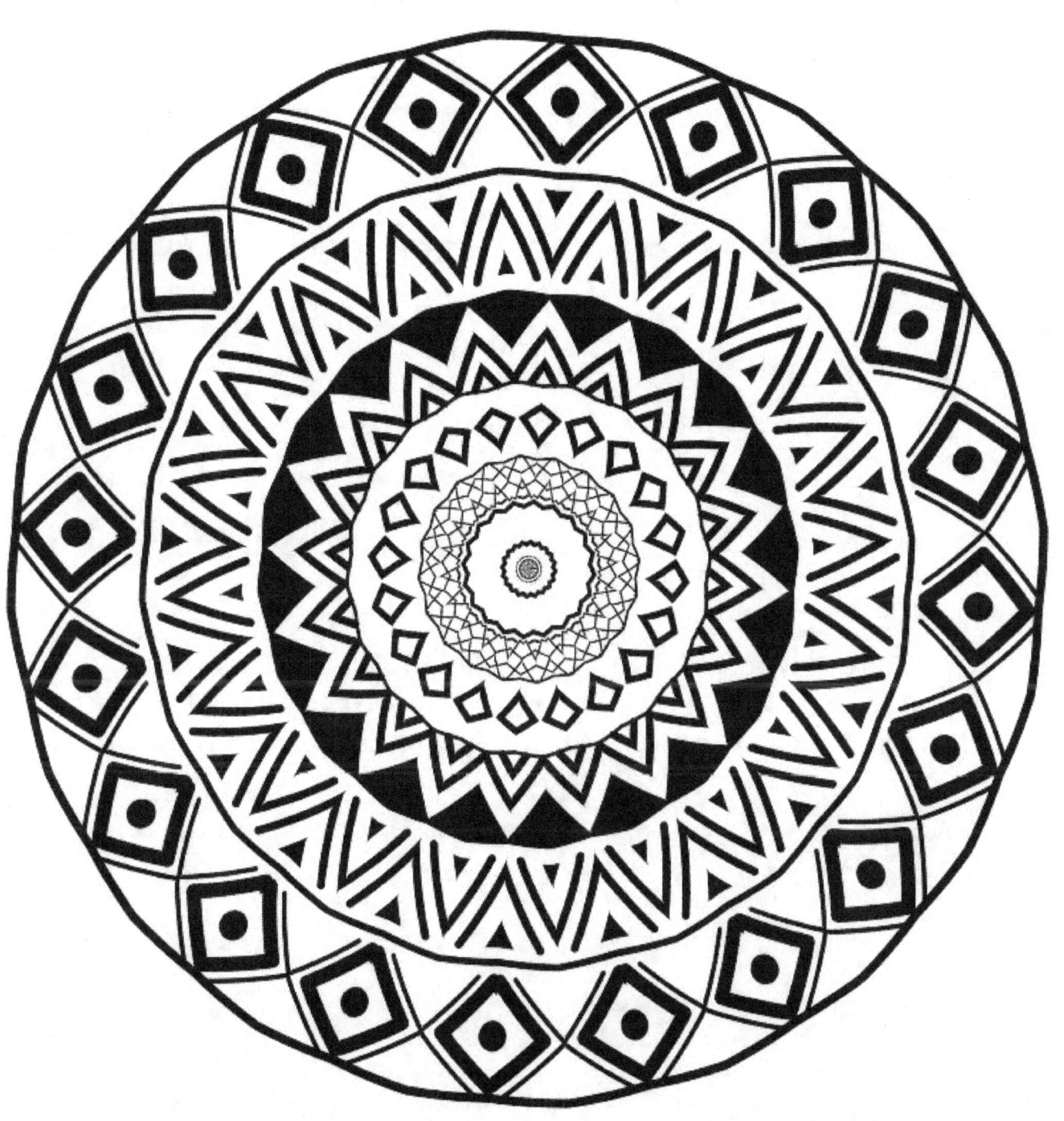

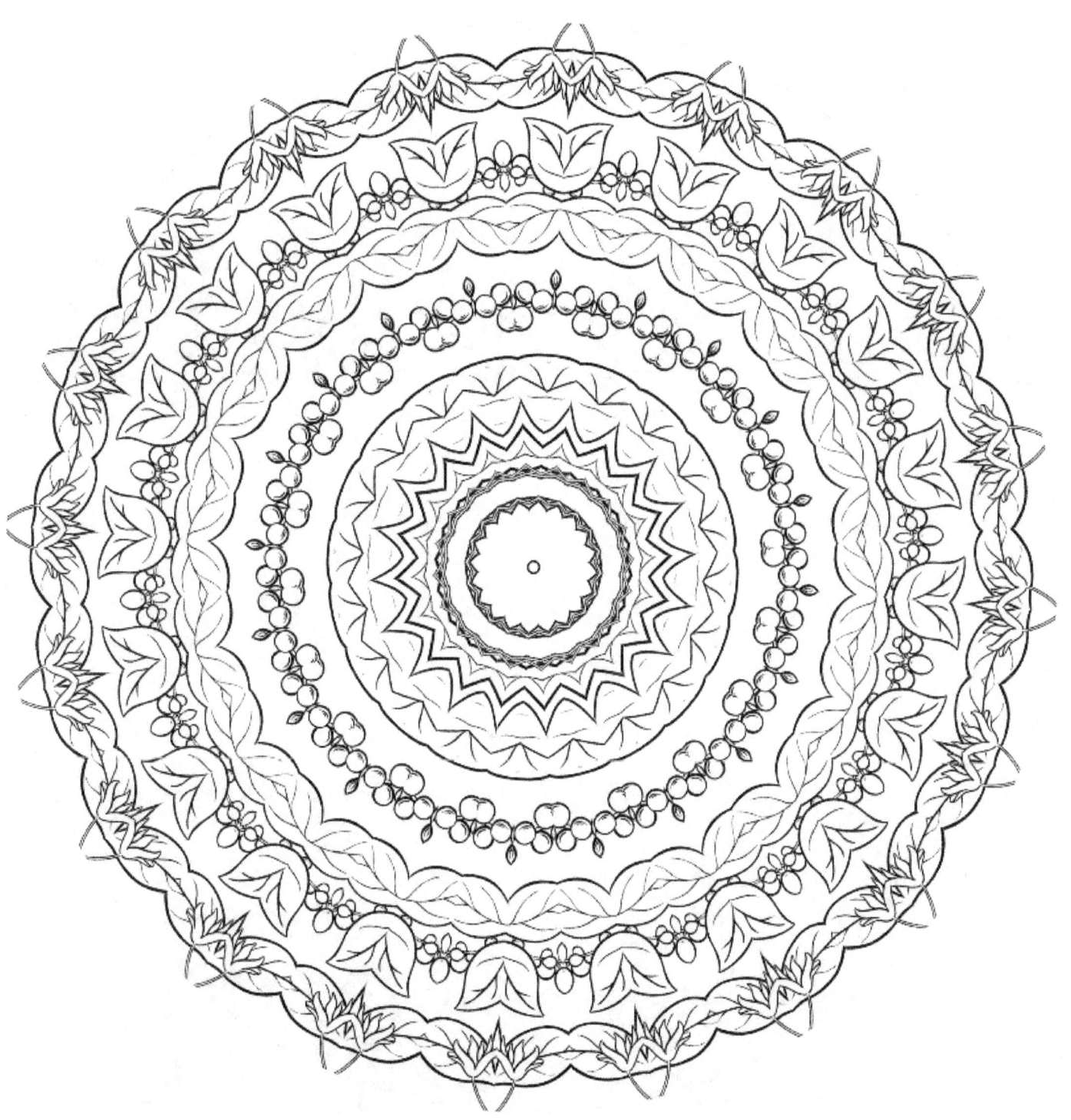

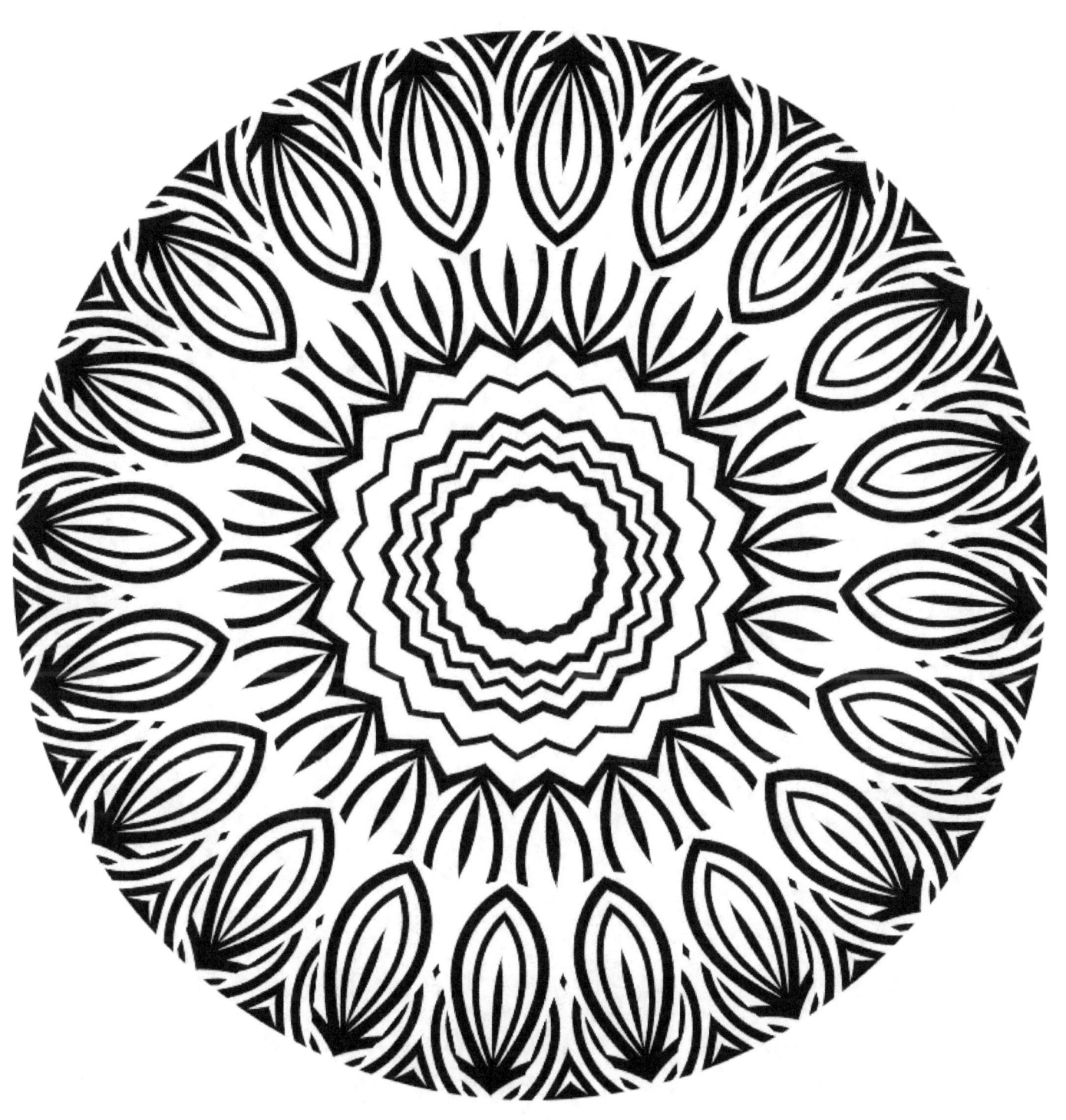

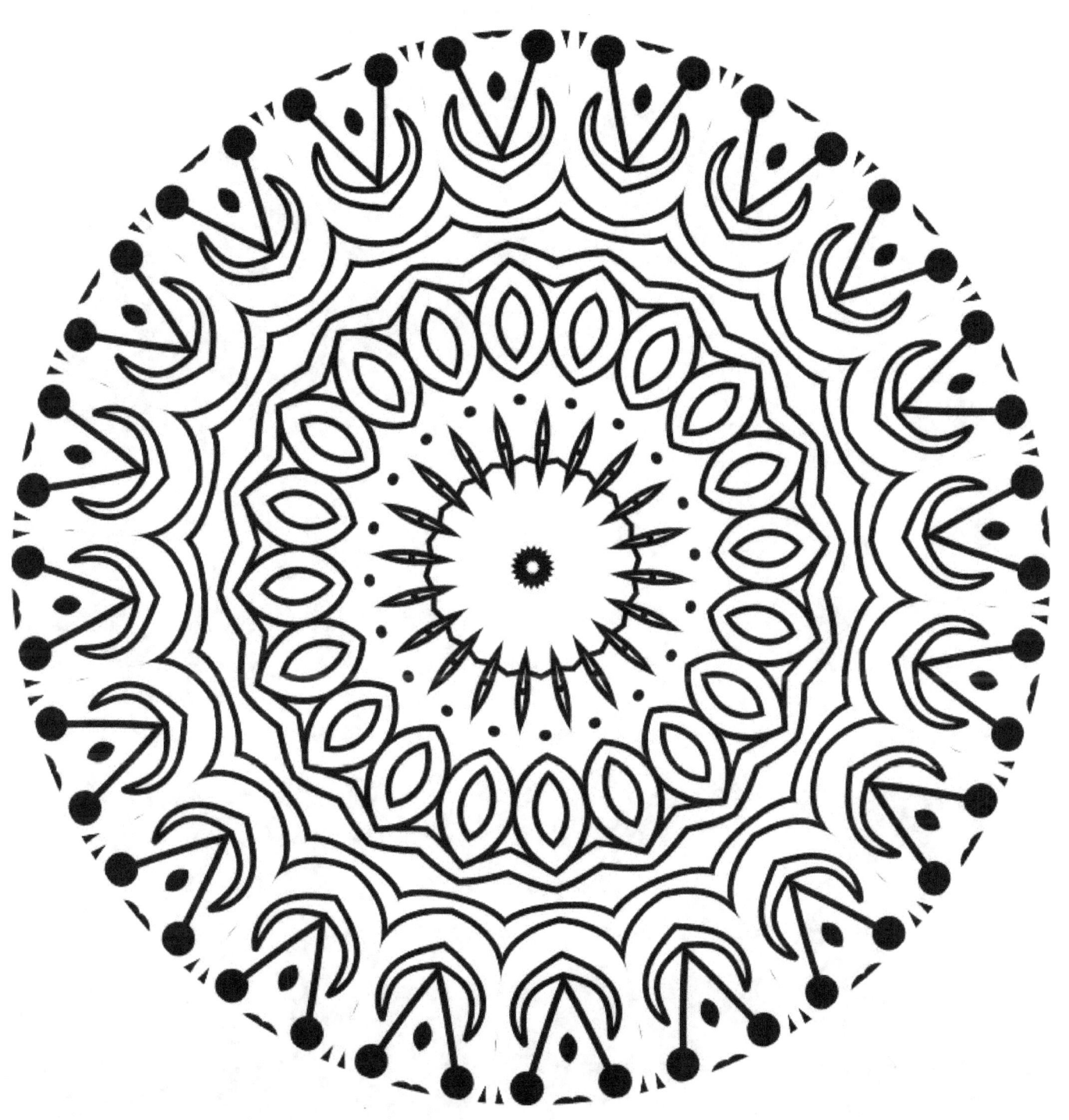

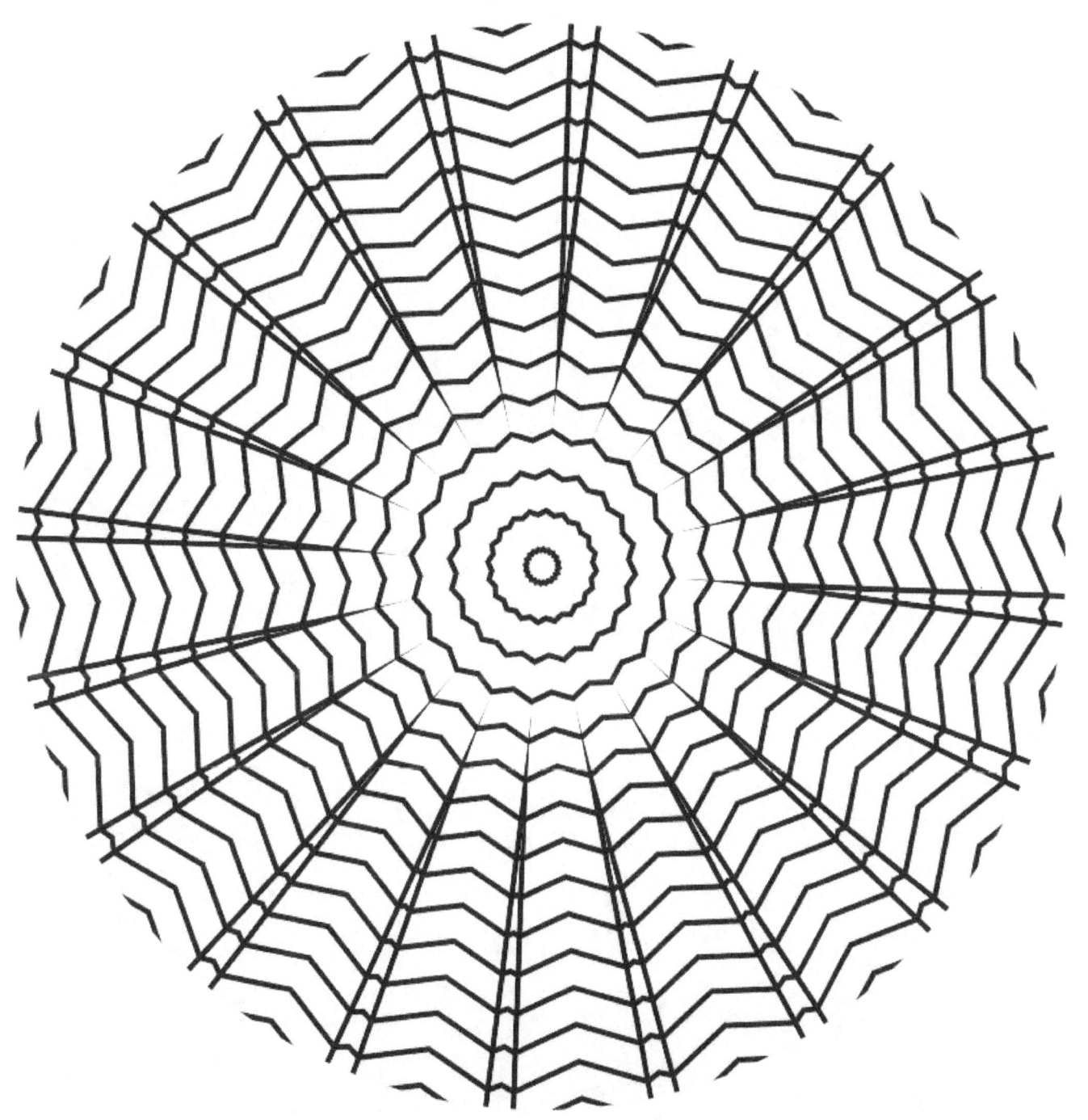

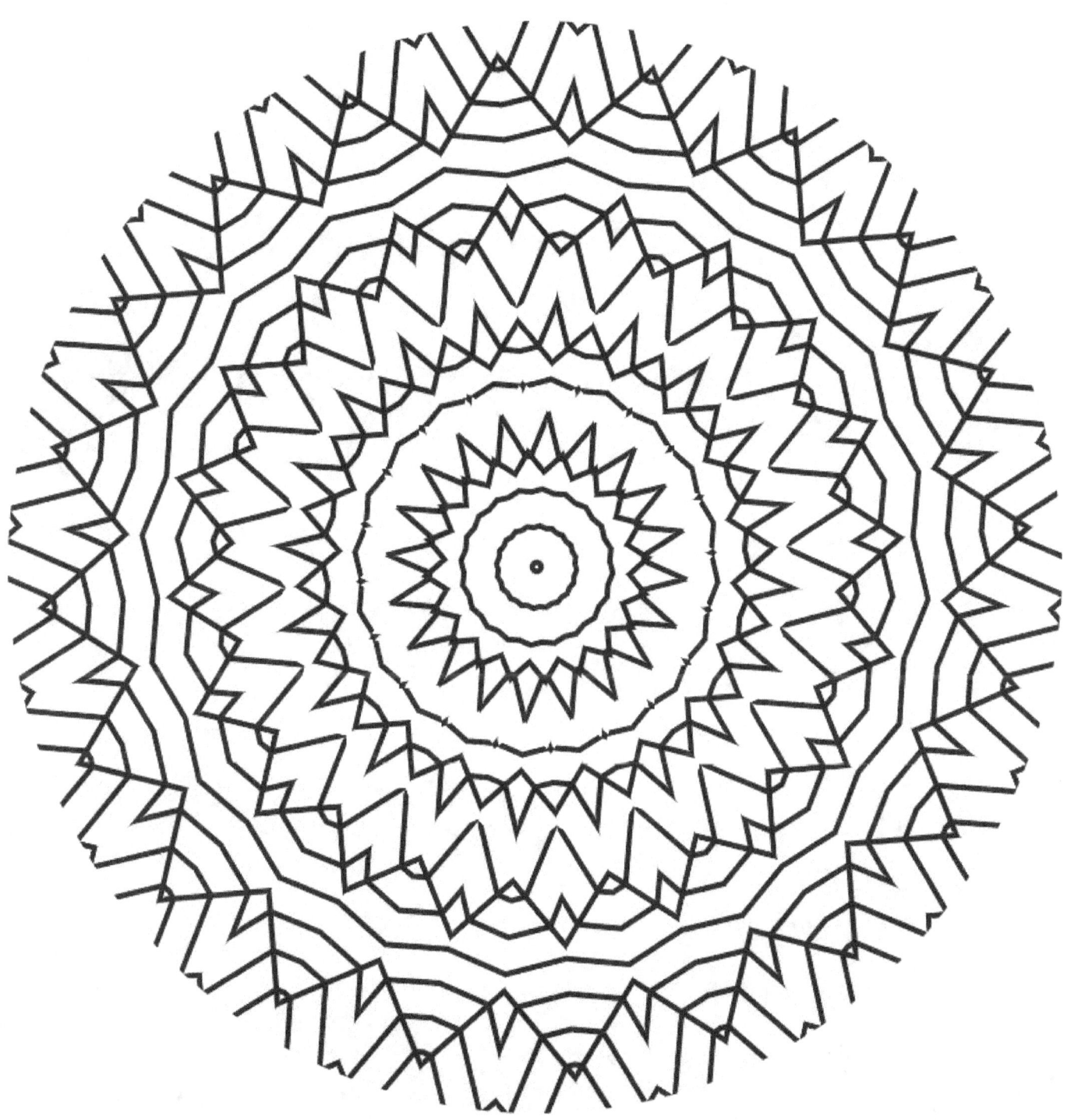

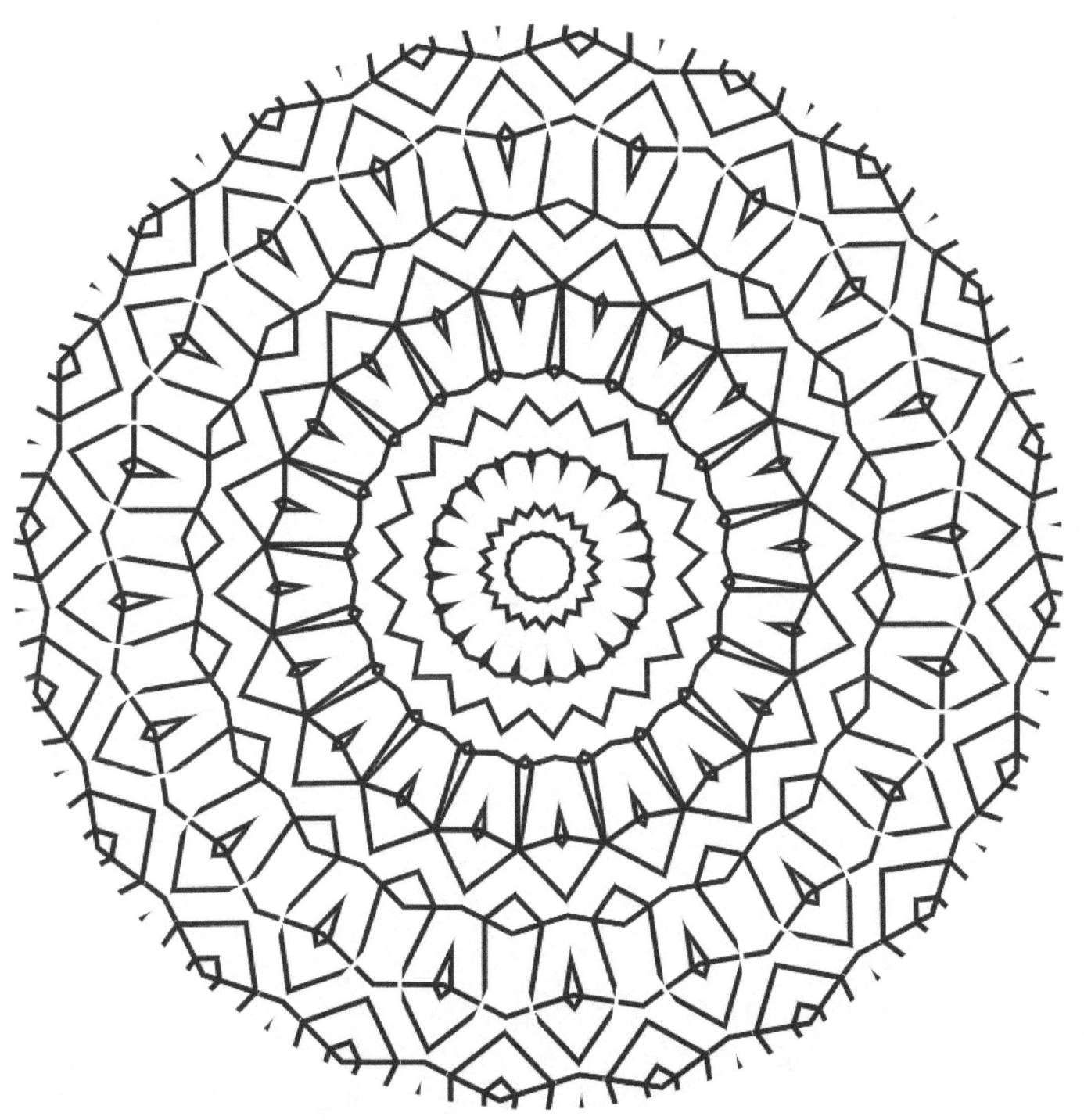

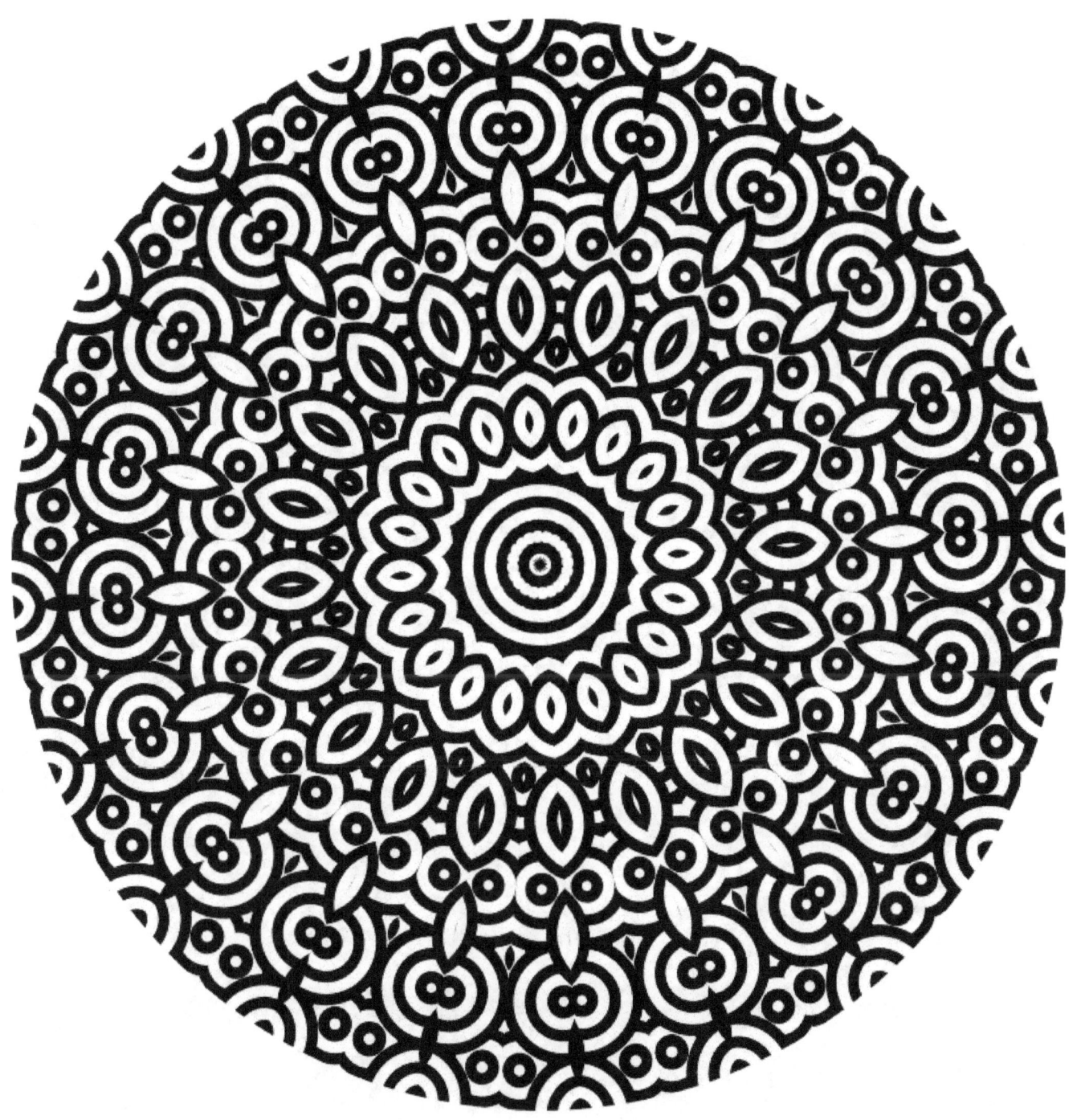

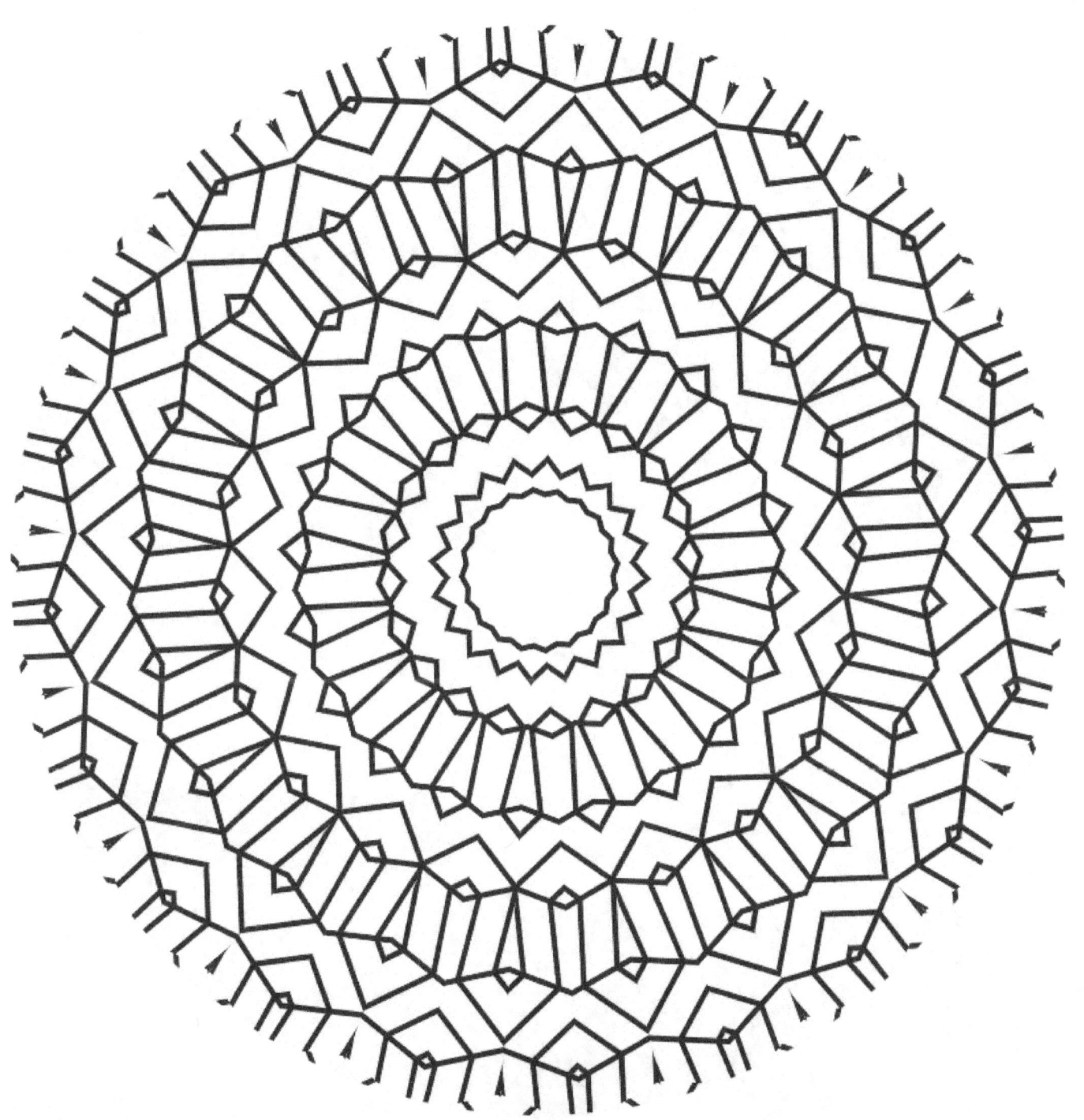

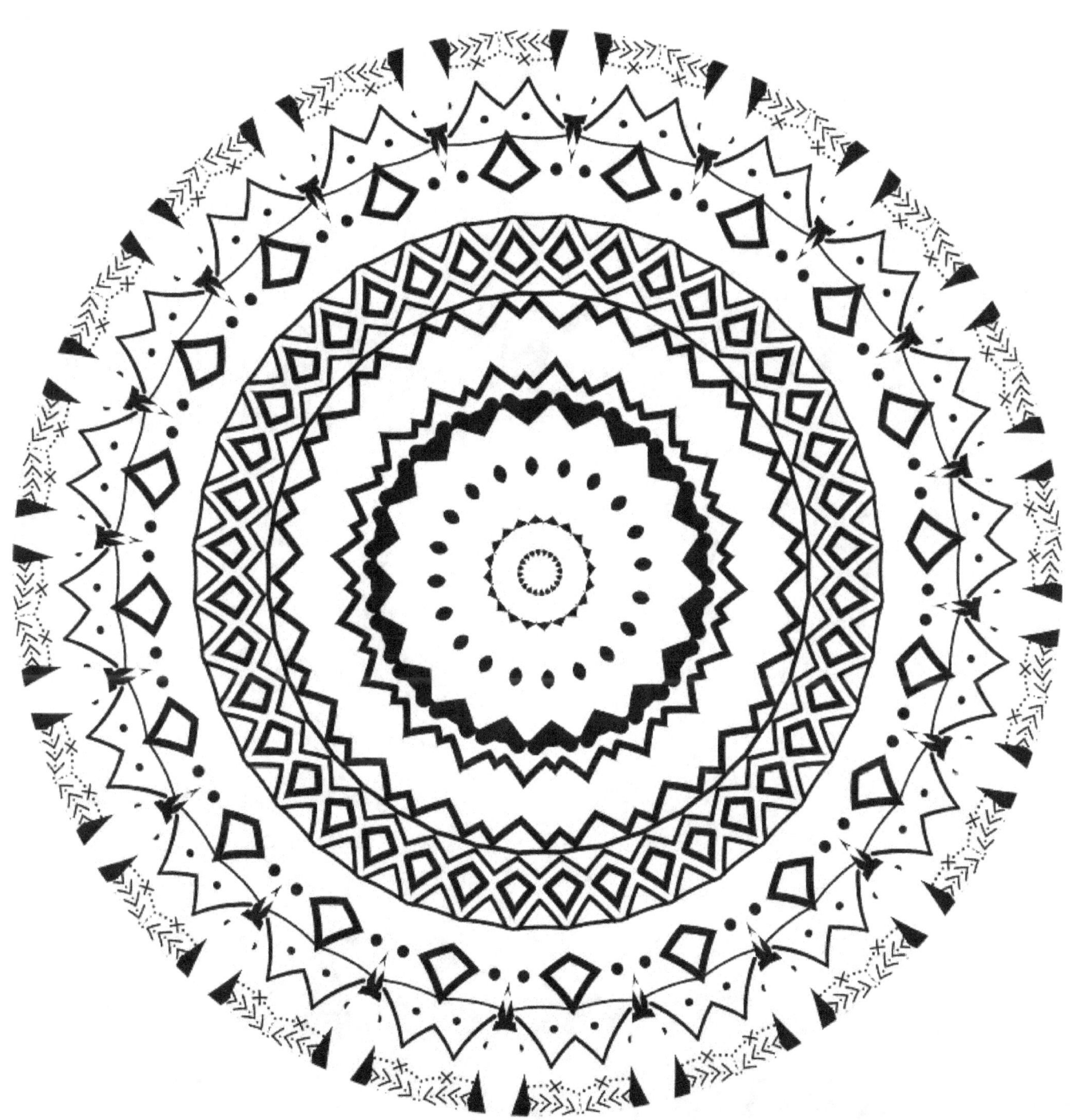

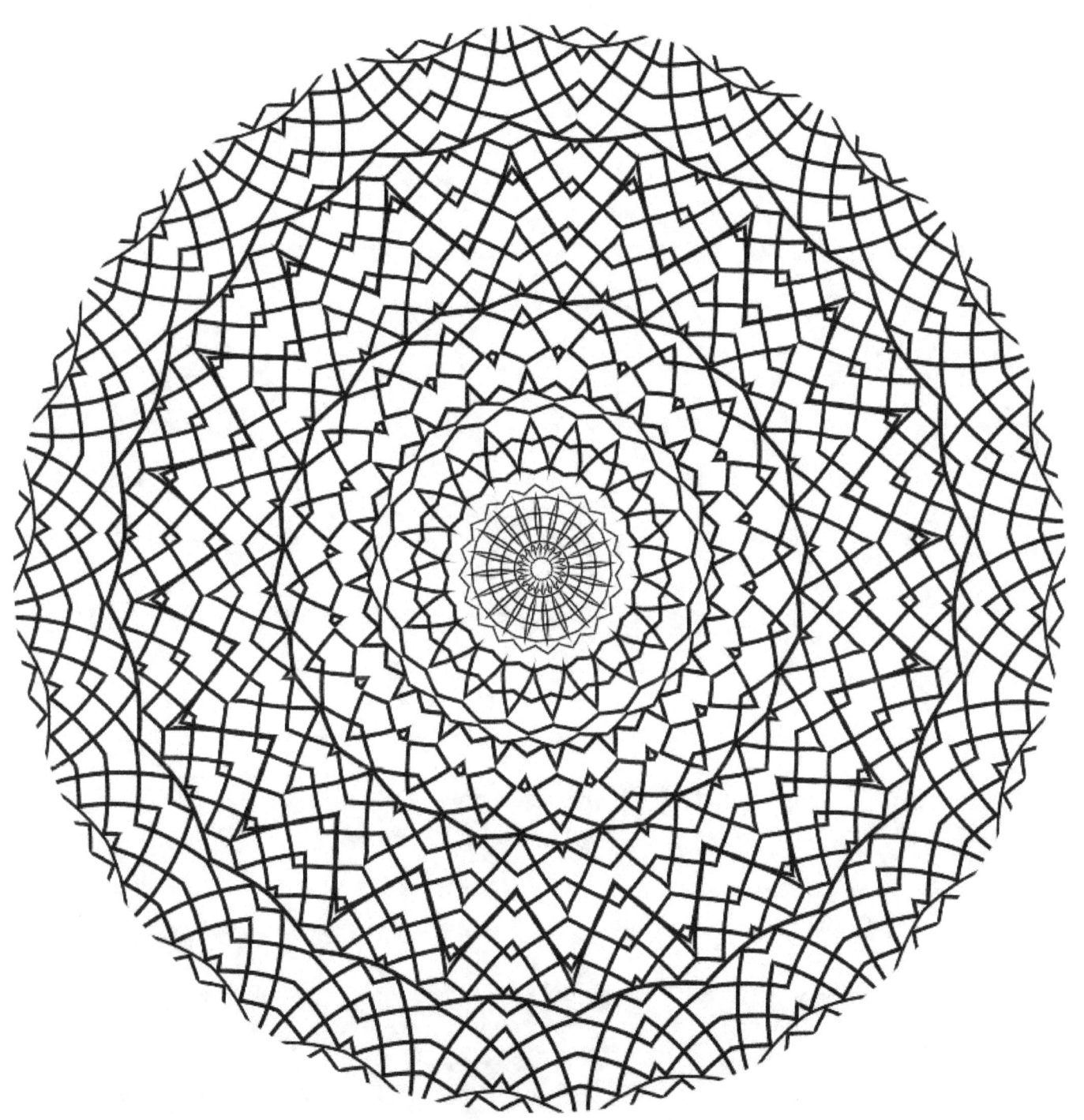

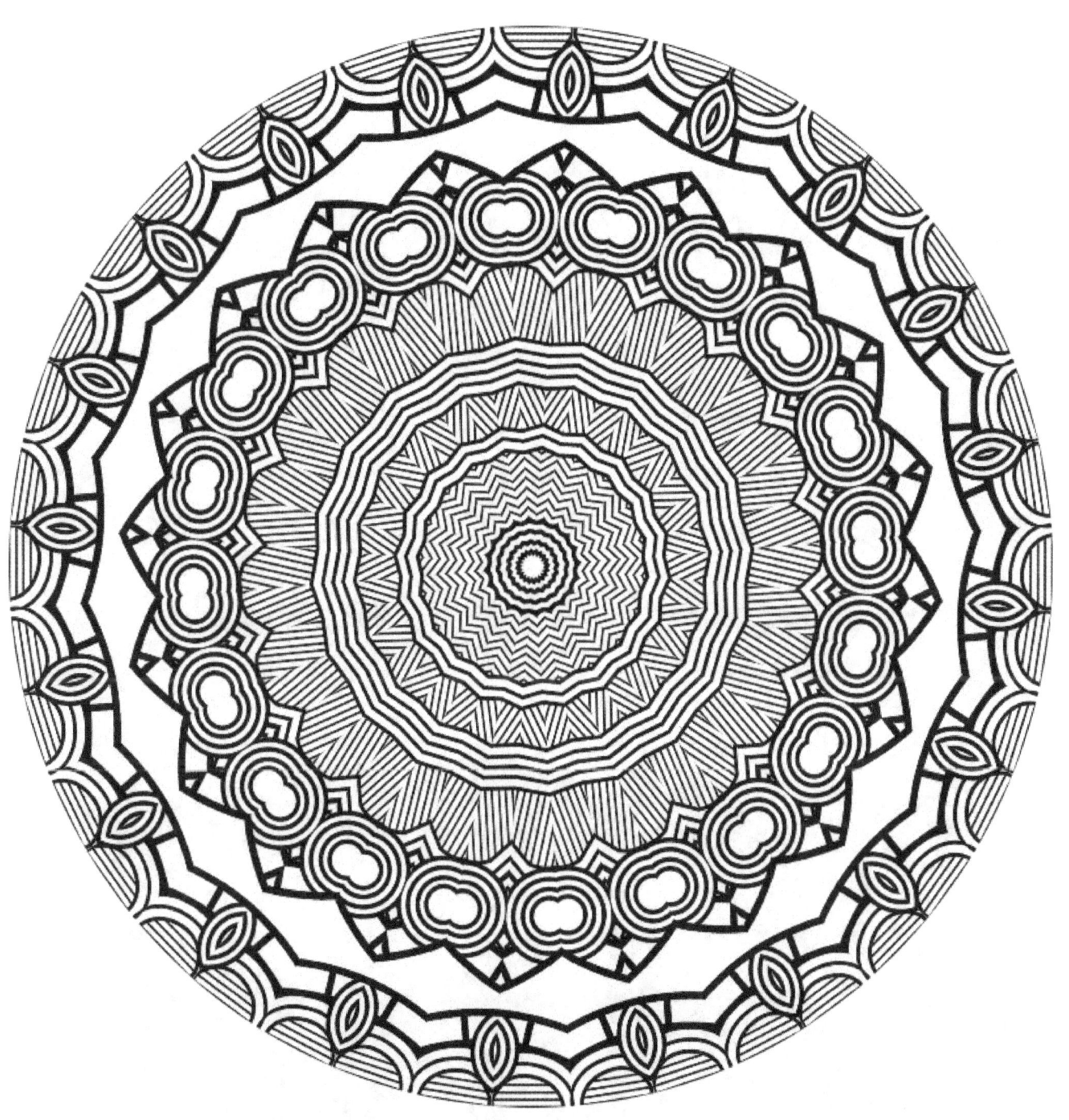

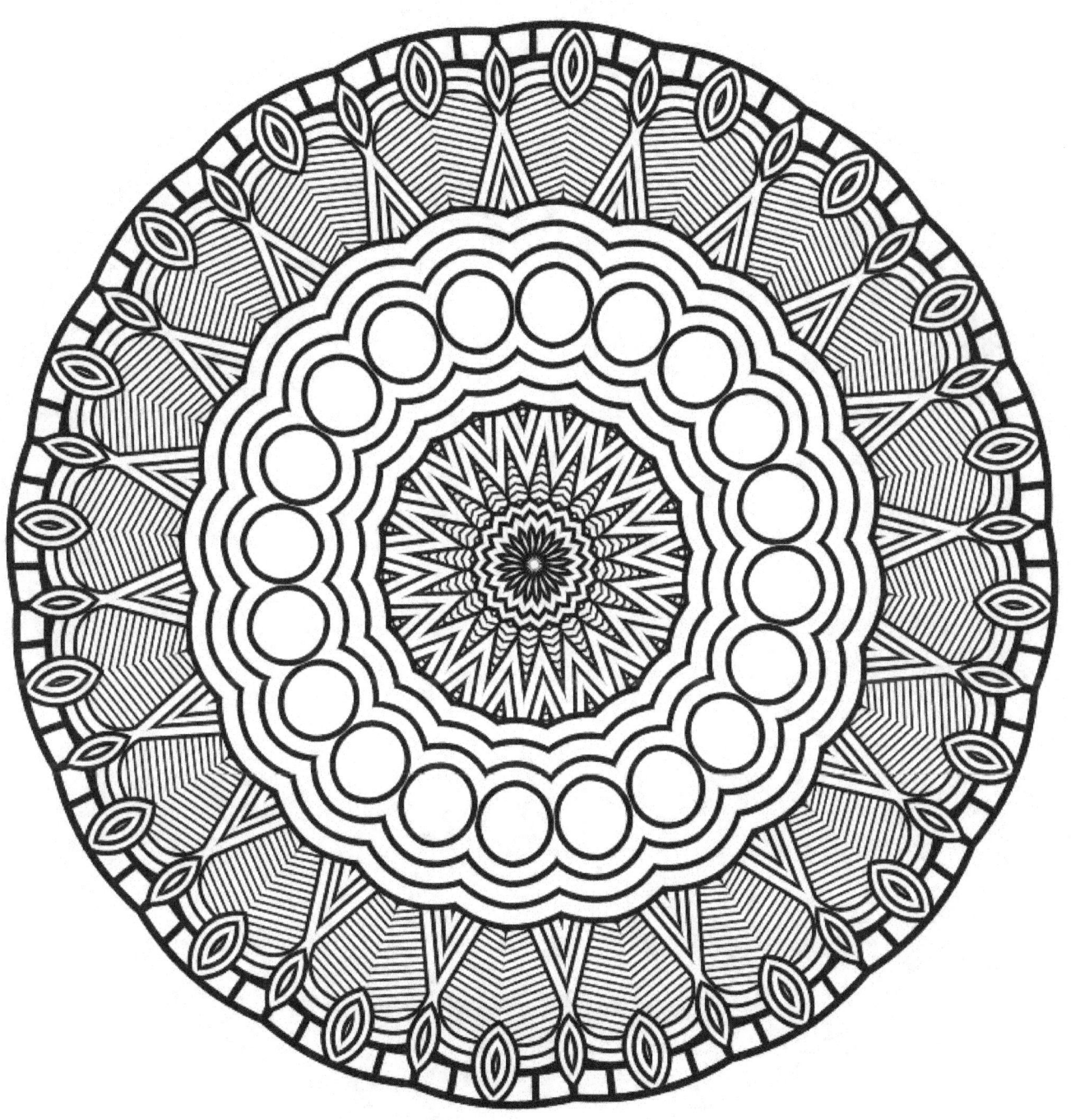

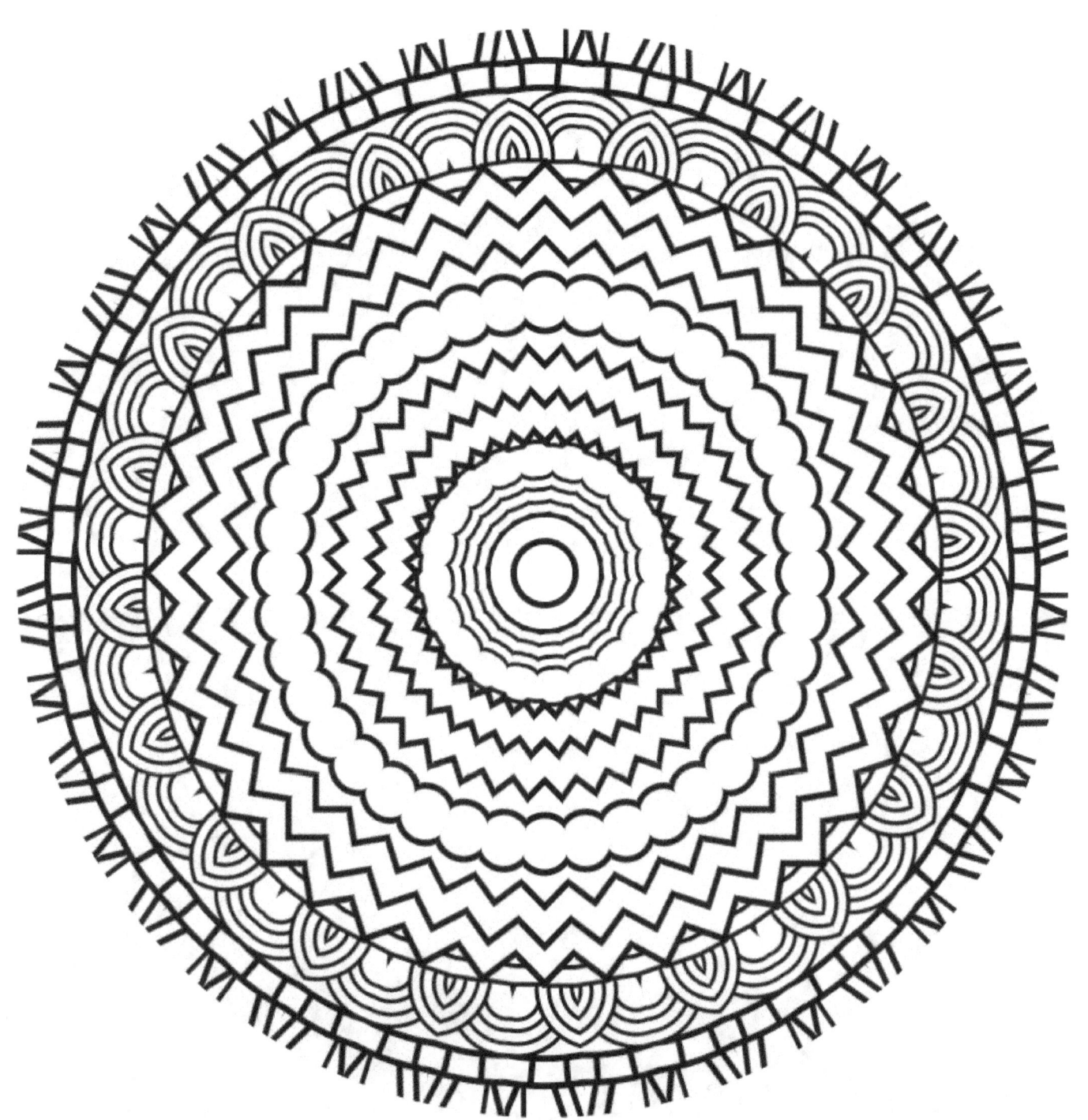

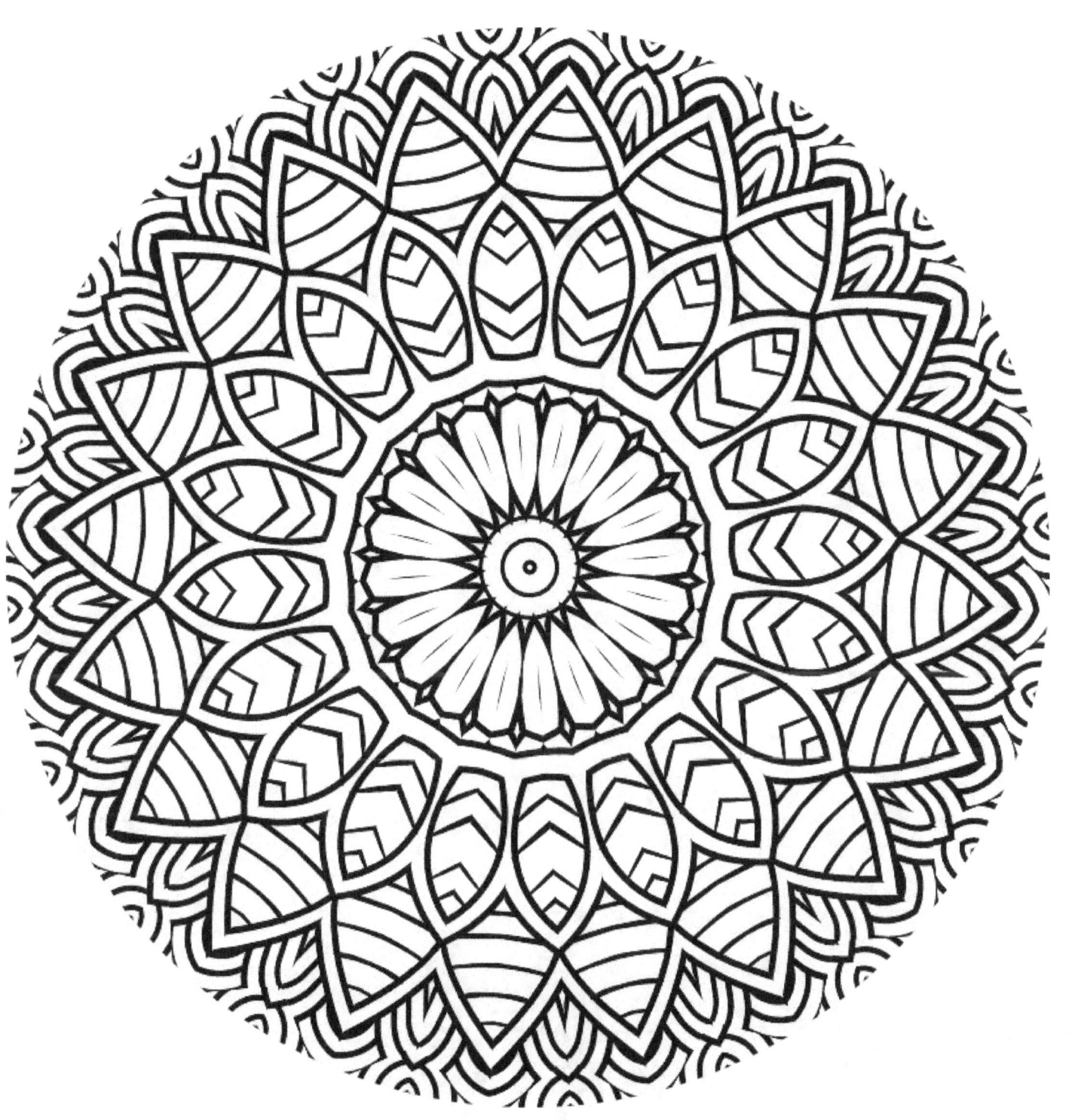

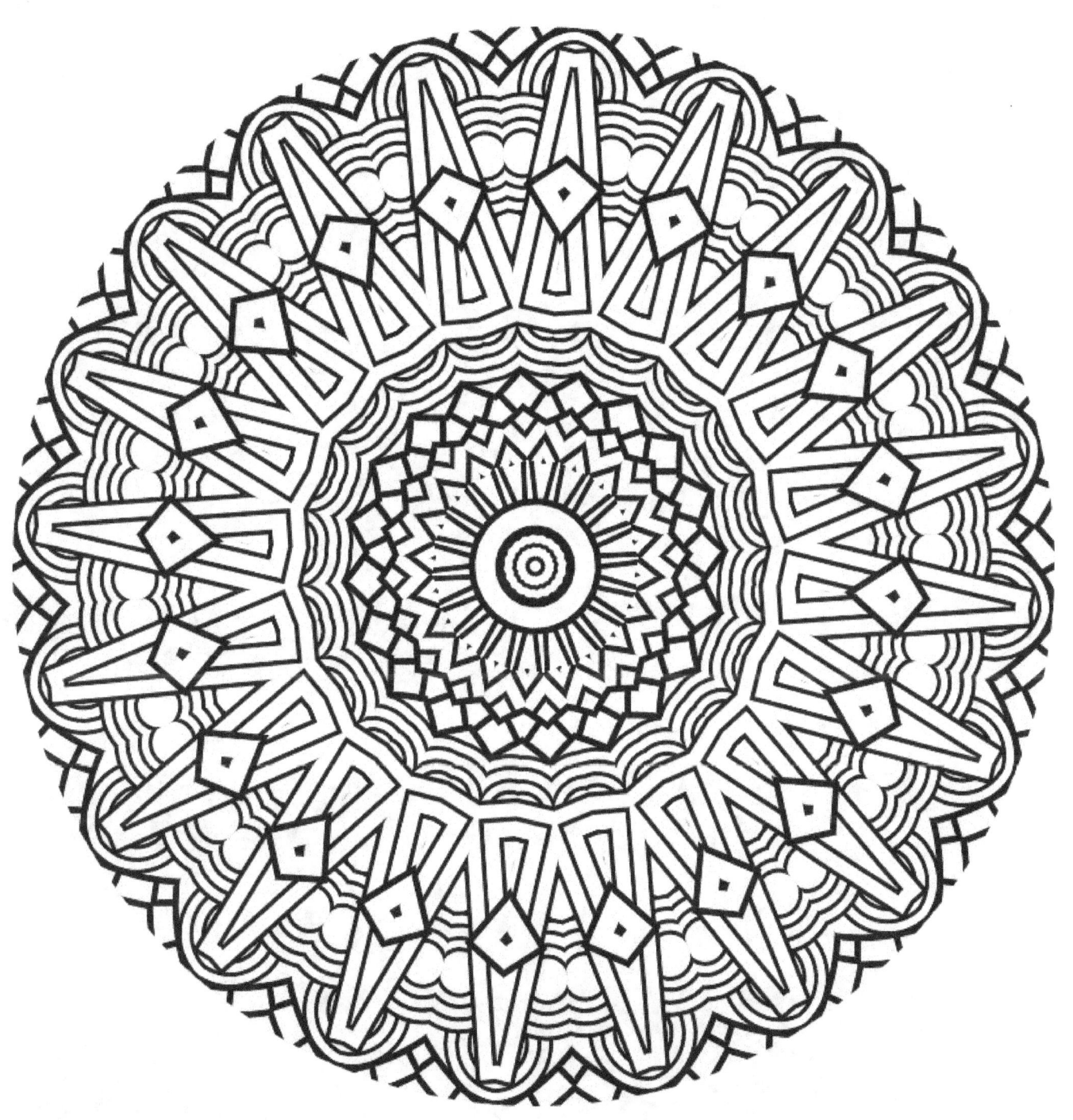

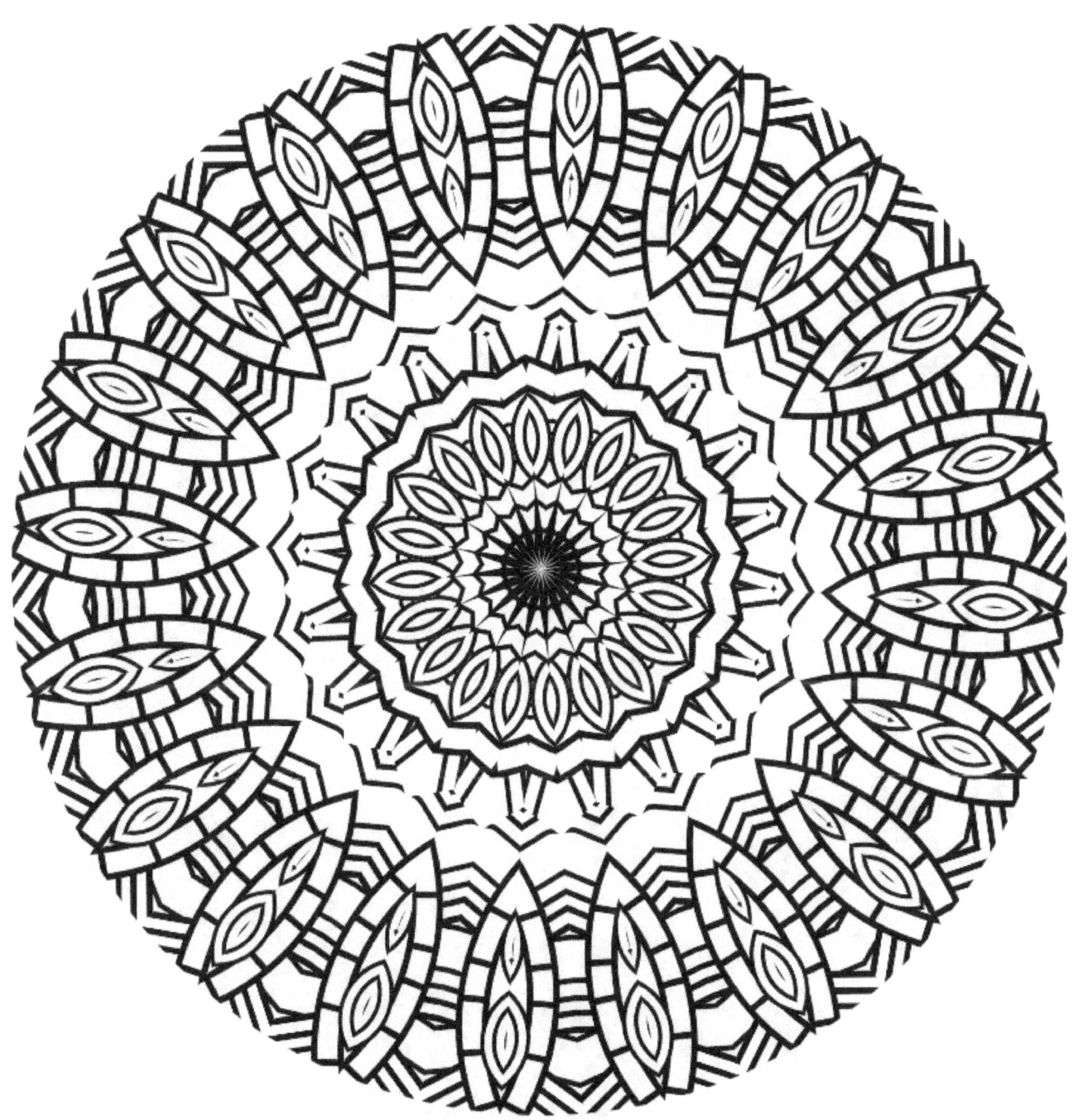

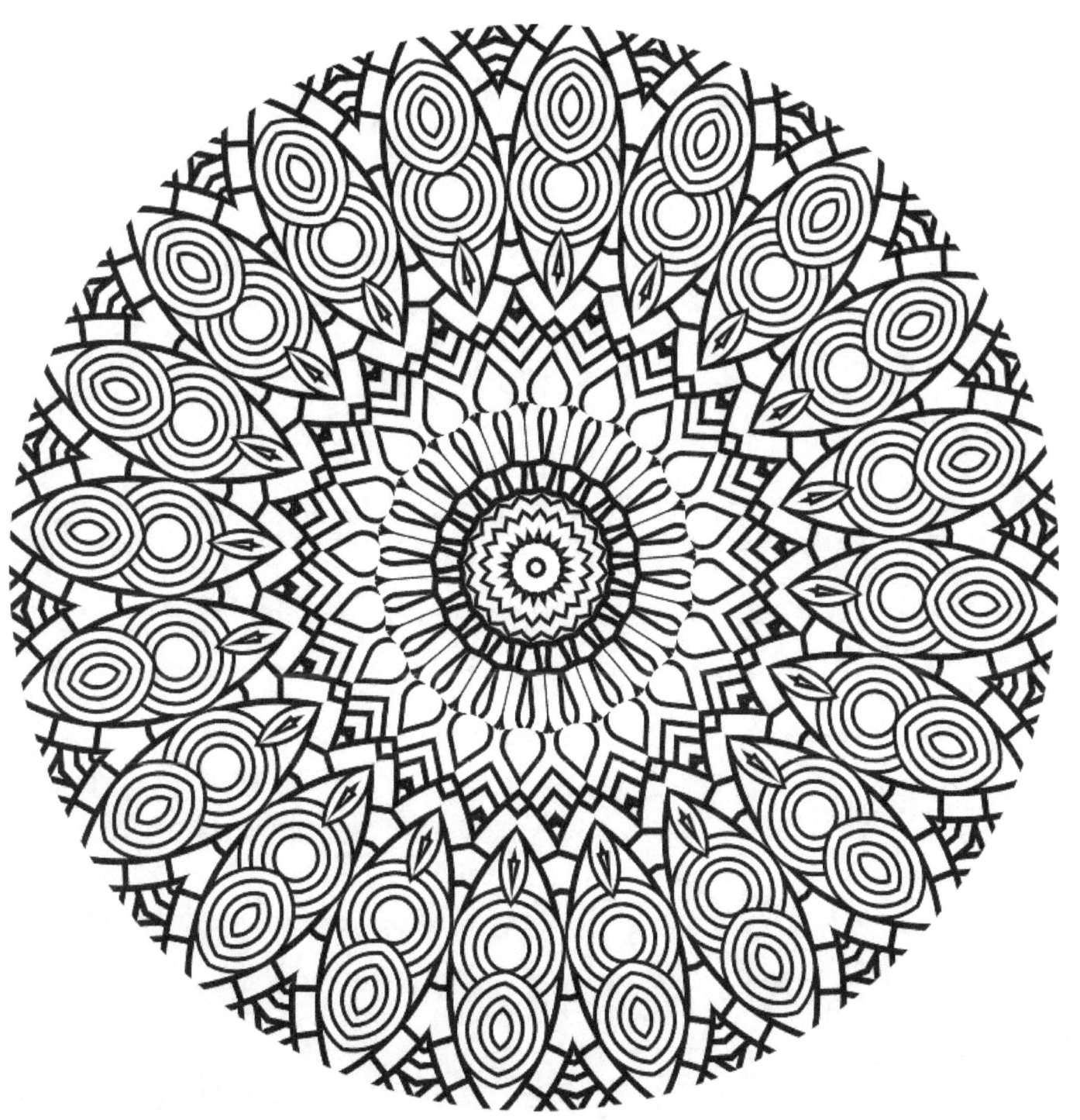

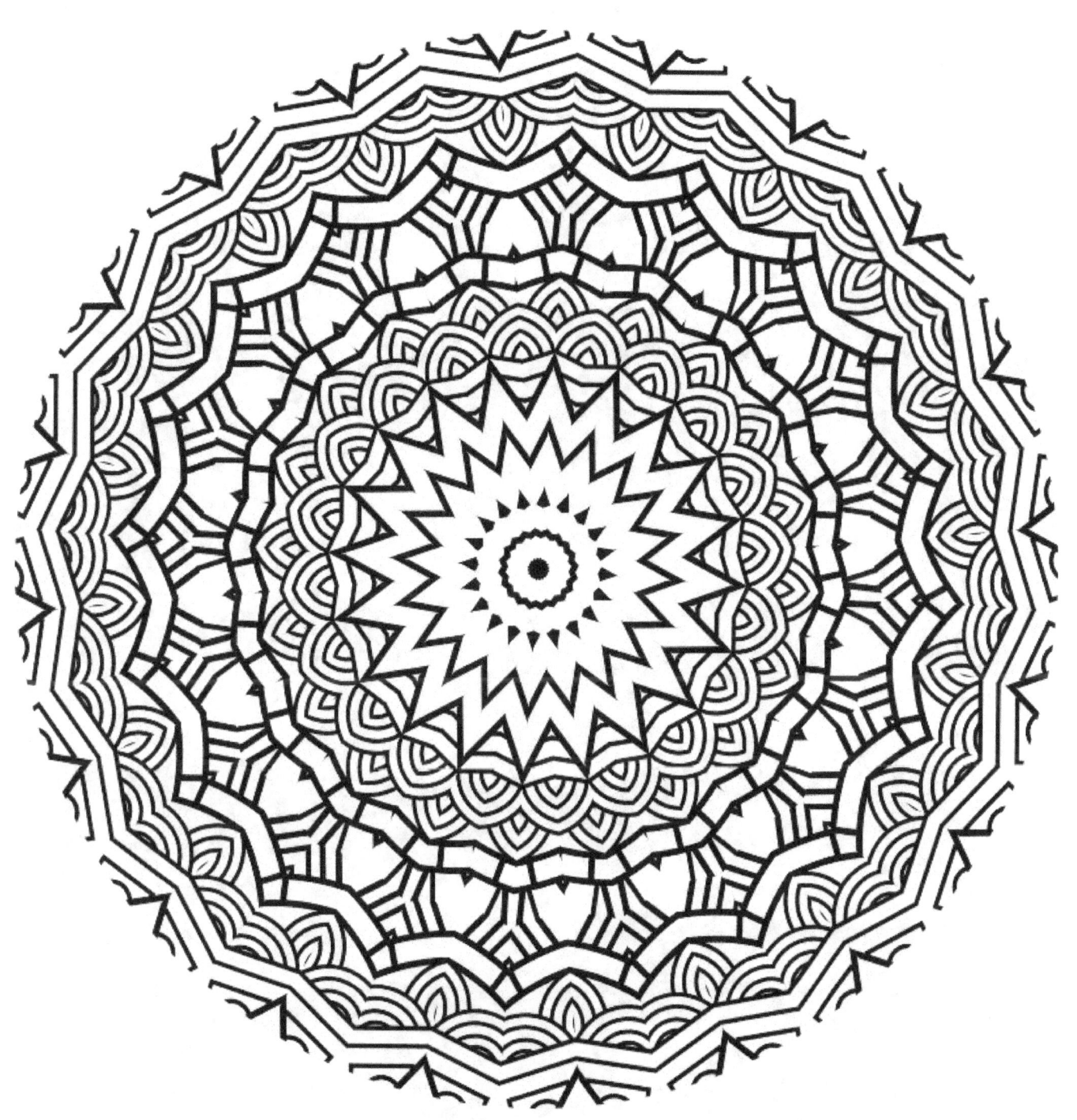

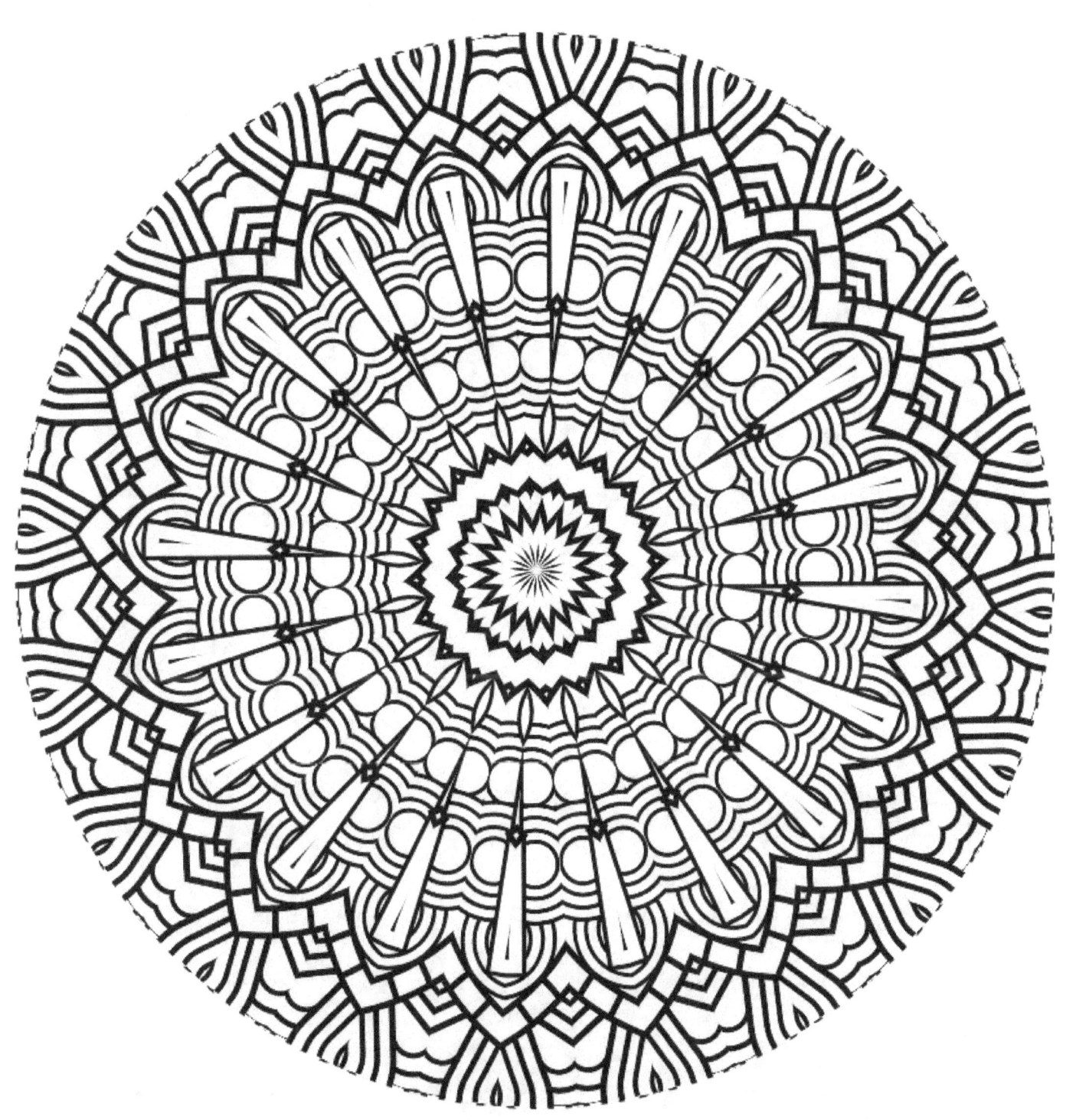

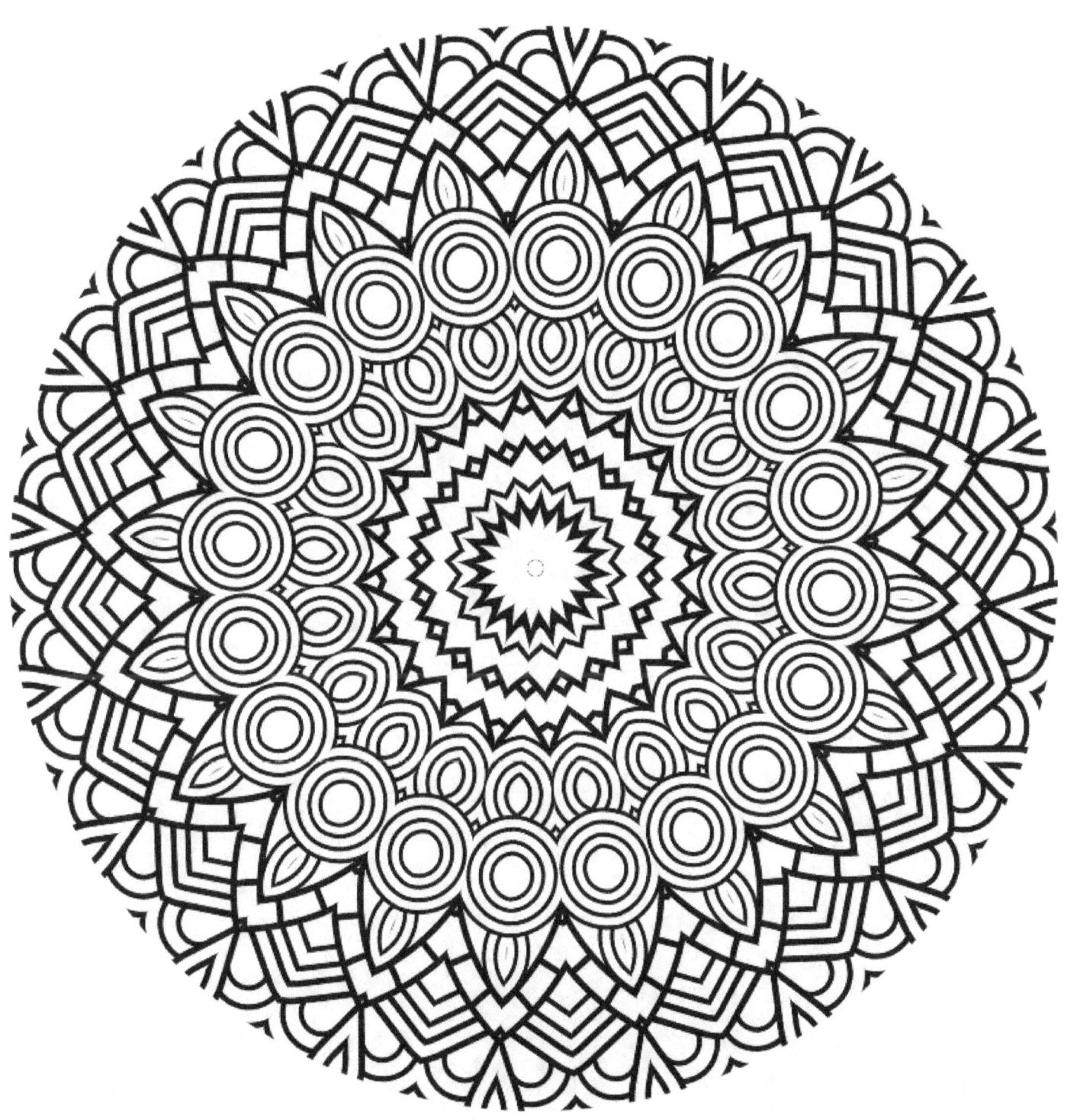

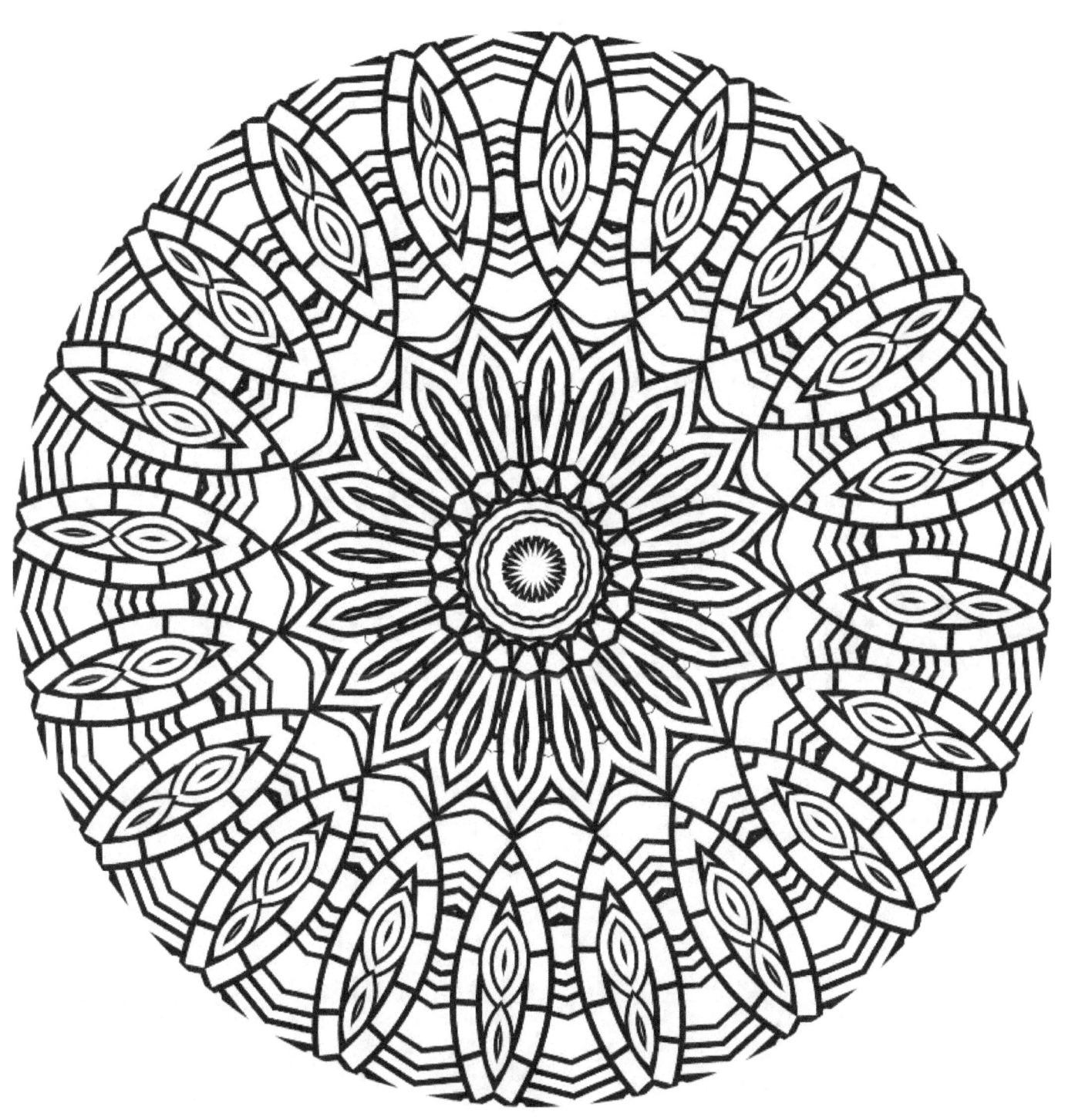

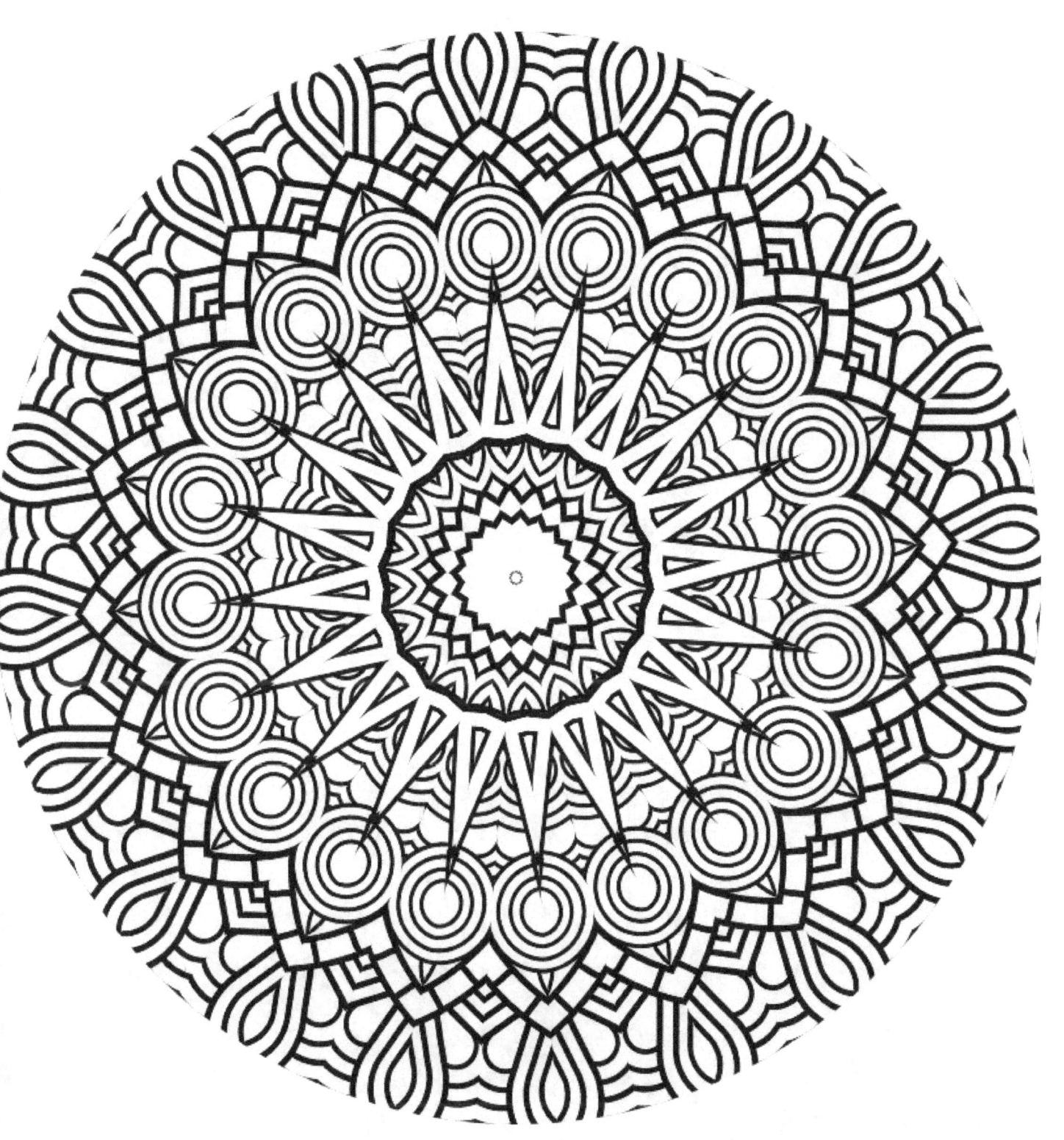

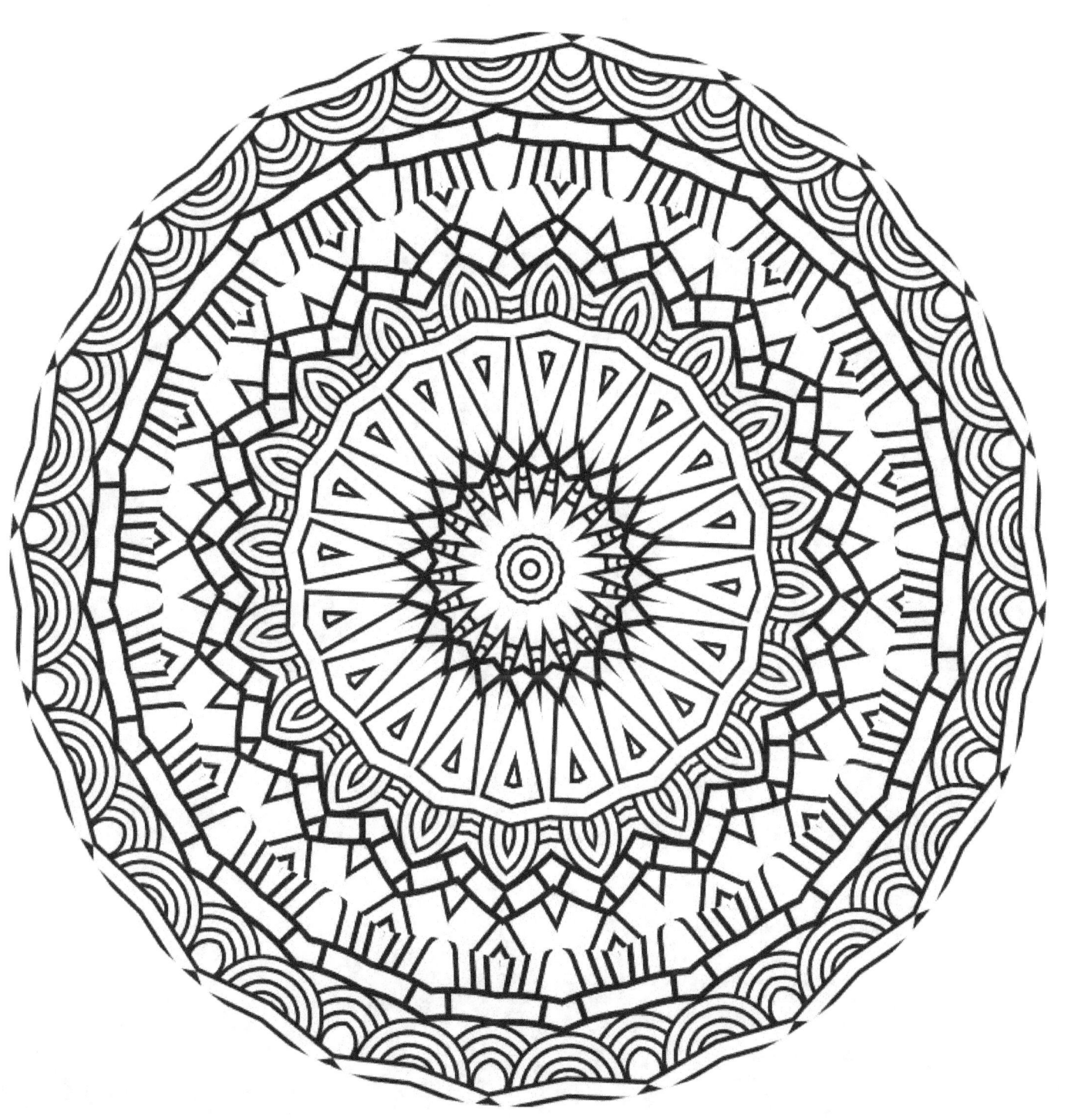

THE END

If you enjoyed coloring this book, please leave us a comment on Amazon Seller's Page and show us your beautiful colors

Email us at
Brainstercornerpublishing @gmail.com
for more freebies!

Thank you